Reading STREET

Grade 2

Scott Foresman

# Fresh Reads
## for Fluency and Comprehension
# Teacher's Manual

Glenview, Illinois

Boston, Massachusetts

Chandler, Arizona

Upper Saddle River, New Jersey

PEARSON

## The Pearson Promise

As the largest educational publishing company in the world, Pearson is committed to providing you with curriculum that not only meets the Common Core State Standards, but also supports your implementation of these standards with your students.

Pearson has aligned the Common Core State Standards to every grade level of *Scott Foresman Reading Street*, our premier educational curriculum. This product provides an alignment of the Common Core State Standards to the Grade 2 assessment items in *Scott Foresman Reading Street Fresh Reads for Fluency and Comprehension*.

We value your partnership highly and look forward to continuing our mission to provide educational materials that fully satisfy your classroom needs.

**PEARSON**

ISBN 13: 978-0-328-72636-3
ISBN 10:     0-328-72636-2

1 2 3 4 5 6 7 8 9 10 V016 21 20 19 18 17 16 15 14 13 12

# Contents

# Unit 4  Our Changing World

# Unit 5  Responsibilities

# Unit 6  Traditions

# NOTES TO THE TEACHER

## Introduction

*Fresh Reads for Fluency and Comprehension* is designed to provide differentiated practice in reading comprehension skills and to prepare children to take the Reading/Language Arts section of standardized tests, state tests, or teacher-made tests. The student book includes the weekly differentiated practice tests to strengthen comprehension skills taught in *Scott Foresman Reading Street*. This Teacher's Manual includes the following: (1) notes on how to use the Fresh Read tests, (2) instructions on how to administer and score a fluency test, (3) two charts on which you may record the progress of your children, and (4) annotated copies of all of the Fresh Read tests indicating the correct answer to all questions.

## How to Use the Fresh Read Tests

The purpose of the Fresh Read tests is to give weekly differentiated practice in target comprehension skills taught in *Scott Foresman Reading Street*.

This book contains three Fresh Read tests for each week to be used independently from the main selection in *Scott Foresman Reading Street*. The tests consist of a "Fresh Read" leveled passage and related comprehension items that focus on the target and review comprehension skills of the week but are written to address varying levels of proficiency—Strategic Intervention (SI), On-Level (OL), and Advanced (A). A code at the bottom of each page tells you the level of each test.

You can assess children's proficiency levels using their responses to discussion questions in class and their work on the comprehension pages in the Reader's and Writer's Notebook. Fresh Read tests can be done independently, or you may choose to work through them with children in small groups, in order to give support and assess children's progress.

Other ways to use the Fresh Read test pages:

- use the Strategic Intervention pages for whole-class practice with the comprehension skills and/or test-taking skills

- use the Strategic Intervention pages after introducing the target and review comprehension skills but prior to reading the main selection in the student anthology of *Scott Foresman Reading Street* to assess children's readiness to read that selection

- use the On-Level pages as an assessment tool to check children's understanding of the comprehension skills and/or test-taking skills

- use the On-Level pages to check children's need for further practice, reteaching, or more challenging materials

- use the Advanced pages as a substitute for the comprehension pages in the Reader's and Writer's Notebook for children working above grade level

- use any of the pages as preparation for the Unit Benchmark Test

# How to Administer and Score a Fluency Test

A fluency test measures a child's reading rate, or the number of words correctly read per minute (wcpm), on grade-level text the child has not seen before. You may want to use a copy of one of the "On-Level" leveled passages from the Fresh Read tests for this purpose. Make a photocopy for yourself of the passage you will give the child. (The pages in this Teacher's Manual have a scale of running numbers to make it easier for you to know how many words the child read during the fluency check, while the passages in the student edition do not have the numbers.) Make sure you have put the child's name and the test date at the top of your copy of the passage. Have a watch or clock with a second hand available for timing the reading.

Give the child a copy of the passage for the test. Note: The child should NOT have seen the passage beforehand; it is a "fresh" reading passage for the child. Do NOT allow the child to read the passage silently before oral reading.

Have the child read the text aloud. Do not have the child read the title as part of the fluency reading; it is not included in the running word count. (You may want to tape-record the child's reading for later evaluation.) Stop the child at exactly one minute and note precisely where the child stopped.

As the child reads orally, on your copy of the text mark any miscues or errors the child makes during the reading (see the chart on page viii). Count the total number of words the child read in one minute. Subtract any words the child read incorrectly. Record the words correct per minute score on the test.

**The formula is:** Total # of words read – # of errors = words correct per minute (wcpm).

You will likely want to keep the test in your folder for the child. You may also want to record children's progress on the Reading Fluency Progress Chart on page xi and/or the Individual Fluency Progress Chart on page xii.

# How to Identify Reading Miscues/Errors

Using the passage on page ix, the chart below shows the kinds of miscues and errors to look for as a child reads aloud and the notations to use to mark them.

| Reading Miscue | Notations |
|---|---|
| **Omission**<br>The child omits words or word parts. | He likes to put his feet in ⟨the⟩ sand. |
| **Substitution**<br>The child substitutes words or parts of words for the words in the text. | He likes to hear the ~~waves.~~ *water* |
| **Insertion**<br>The child inserts words or parts of words that are not in the text. | He likes to see the birds ⌃*fly* in the sky. |
| **Mispronunciation/Misreading**<br>The child pronounces or reads a word incorrectly. | Zhou saw the face ~~going~~ *growing* up and down in the waves. |
| **Hesitation**<br>The child hesitates over a word and the teacher provides the word. | *H*<br><u>Zhou</u> likes to be near the ocean. |
| **Self-correction**<br>The child reads a word incorrectly but then corrects the error. | One day, Zhou saw a li*ttle* ⟨sc⟩ face in the water. |

## Notes

- If the child hesitates over a word, wait several seconds before telling the child what the word is.

- If a child makes the same error more than once, count it as only one error.

- Self-correction is not counted as an actual error. However, writing "SC" over the word or words will help you identify words that give the child some difficulty.

## Sample Fluency Test

Here is the passage marked as shown on the previous page. This is the "On-Level" passage from Grade 2, Unit 1, Week 1. As the child reads the passage aloud to you, mark miscues and errors. Have the child read for exactly one minute, and then mark the last word the child reads.

Name *Susan*     *9/4/2009*   (62)                    **The Twin Club**

### What Is It?

*H*
Zhou likes to be near the ocean. He likes to hear the ~~waves~~ *water*. He likes     | 15

to put his feet in (the) sand. He likes to see the birds *fly*^ in the sky.     | 31

One day, Zhou saw a (sc) little face in the water. The face was dark gray.     | 46

The face had black eyes and a long nose like a dog. Zhou saw the face     | 62

*growing*
going up and down in | the waves.     | 69

"Look! Look!" Zhou said to Mom.     | 75

Mom stopped reading her book.     | 80

"What is it?" Zhou asked.     | 85

"It is a seal," Mom said. "Seals like to swim in the ocean. They look     | 100

for fish to eat in the water."     | 107

"I like to swim in the ocean too!" Zhou said.     | 117

*67 - 5 = 62*

Total number of words read    **67**
Number of errors        **– 5**
_____
Words correct per minute    **62**

# Interpreting the Results

According to published norms for oral reading fluency, children at the end of Grade 2 should be reading fluently at 90 words correct per minute in text that is on grade level. This chart gives recommended progress toward that goal.

| End of Unit/Grade | | Reading Rate (wcpm) |
| --- | --- | --- |
| Grade 2 | Unit 1 | 40 to 50 |
| Grade 2 | Unit 2 | 48 to 58 |
| Grade 2 | Unit 3 | 55 to 65 |
| Grade 2 | Unit 4 | 62 to 72 |
| Grade 2 | Unit 5 | 70 to 82 |
| Grade 2 | Unit 6 | 80 to 90 |
| End-of-Year Goal | | 90 |

If a child's reading rate is lower than the suggested progress toward the standard for his or her grade level, your notes on the child's miscues may help you determine why the rate is low. Does the child make errors that indicate his or her decoding skills are poor? If so, further instruction in phonics may be needed. Do the errors reflect a lack of comprehension or limited vocabulary? In that case, instruction in comprehension strategies and exposure to more vocabulary words may help. A lack of fluency may indicate a lack of exposure to models of fluent oral reading. It may also mean that the child isn't reading enough material at his or her reading level. Encourage the child to read more books or children's magazine articles at an accessible or comfortable level of reading for him or her.

# Reading Fluency Progress Chart

| Child's Name | Unit 1 | | Unit 2 | | Unit 3 | | Unit 4 | | Unit 5 | | Unit 6 | |
|---|---|---|---|---|---|---|---|---|---|---|---|---|
| | Date | WCPM | Date | WCPM | Date | WCPM | Date | WCPM | Date | WCPM | Date | WCPM |
| 1. | | | | | | | | | | | | |
| 2. | | | | | | | | | | | | |
| 3. | | | | | | | | | | | | |
| 4. | | | | | | | | | | | | |
| 5. | | | | | | | | | | | | |
| 6. | | | | | | | | | | | | |
| 7. | | | | | | | | | | | | |
| 8. | | | | | | | | | | | | |
| 9. | | | | | | | | | | | | |
| 10. | | | | | | | | | | | | |
| 11. | | | | | | | | | | | | |
| 12. | | | | | | | | | | | | |
| 13. | | | | | | | | | | | | |
| 14. | | | | | | | | | | | | |
| 15. | | | | | | | | | | | | |
| 16. | | | | | | | | | | | | |
| 17. | | | | | | | | | | | | |
| 18. | | | | | | | | | | | | |
| 19. | | | | | | | | | | | | |
| 20. | | | | | | | | | | | | |
| 21. | | | | | | | | | | | | |
| 22. | | | | | | | | | | | | |
| 23. | | | | | | | | | | | | |
| 24. | | | | | | | | | | | | |
| 25. | | | | | | | | | | | | |
| 26. | | | | | | | | | | | | |
| 27. | | | | | | | | | | | | |
| 28. | | | | | | | | | | | | |
| 29. | | | | | | | | | | | | |
| 30. | | | | | | | | | | | | |
| 31. | | | | | | | | | | | | |
| 32. | | | | | | | | | | | | |
| 33. | | | | | | | | | | | | |
| 34. | | | | | | | | | | | | |
| 35. | | | | | | | | | | | | |

# Individual Fluency Progress Chart, Grade 2

Name _____

| WCPM | 1 | 2 | 3 | 4 | 5 | 6 | 7 | 8 | 9 | 10 | 11 | 12 | 13 | 14 | 15 | 16 | 17 | 18 | 19 | 20 | 21 | 22 | 23 | 24 | 25 | 26 | 27 | 28 | 29 | 30 |
|---|---|---|---|---|---|---|---|---|---|---|---|---|---|---|---|---|---|---|---|---|---|---|---|---|---|---|---|---|---|---|
| 125 | | | | | | | | | | | | | | | | | | | | | | | | | | | | | | |
| 120 | | | | | | | | | | | | | | | | | | | | | | | | | | | | | | |
| 115 | | | | | | | | | | | | | | | | | | | | | | | | | | | | | | |
| 110 | | | | | | | | | | | | | | | | | | | | | | | | | | | | | | |
| 105 | | | | | | | | | | | | | | | | | | | | | | | | | | | | | | |
| 100 | | | | | | | | | | | | | | | | | | | | | | | | | | | | | | |
| 95 | | | | | | | | | | | | | | | | | | | | | | | | | | | | | | |
| 90 | | | | | | | | | | | | | | | | | | | | | | | | | | | | | | |
| 85 | | | | | | | | | | | | | | | | | | | | | | | | | | | | | | |
| 80 | | | | | | | | | | | | | | | | | | | | | | | | | | | | | | |
| 75 | | | | | | | | | | | | | | | | | | | | | | | | | | | | | | |
| 70 | | | | | | | | | | | | | | | | | | | | | | | | | | | | | | |
| 65 | | | | | | | | | | | | | | | | | | | | | | | | | | | | | | |
| 60 | | | | | | | | | | | | | | | | | | | | | | | | | | | | | | |
| 55 | | | | | | | | | | | | | | | | | | | | | | | | | | | | | | |
| 50 | | | | | | | | | | | | | | | | | | | | | | | | | | | | | | |
| 45 | | | | | | | | | | | | | | | | | | | | | | | | | | | | | | |
| 40 | | | | | | | | | | | | | | | | | | | | | | | | | | | | | | |
| 35 | | | | | | | | | | | | | | | | | | | | | | | | | | | | | | |
| 30 | | | | | | | | | | | | | | | | | | | | | | | | | | | | | | |

Timed Reading/Week

**Fresh Reads for Fluency and Comprehension**

Name _____

**Read the selection. Then answer the questions that follow.**

### A Great Day

| | |
|---|---|
| Oscar and Emma went to the zoo. They went with their father. It was | 14 |
| a nice day. The animals were playing in the sun. | 24 |
| "Look! Here are the monkeys!" Oscar said. | 31 |
| "I want to see the lions!" Emma said. | 39 |
| "Yes," said Dad, "and we can see the bears too!" | 49 |
| They had a great day at the zoo. | 57 |

**Turn the page.**

**Answer the questions below.**

**1** **Which sentence tells about Oscar and Emma?**

○ They did not like to be outside.

● They were excited about their day.

○ They were afraid of the bears.

**2** **Where does this story take place?**

● at the zoo

○ at home

○ at school

**3** **What is this story mostly about?**

○ learning about monkeys

○ going home after a great day

● seeing animals at the zoo

**4** **What do Oscar, Emma, and Dad like to do together?**

# Possible response: They like going to the zoo together.

**Common Core State Standards**

**Questions 1, 2, 4: Literature 1.** Ask and answer such questions as *who, what, where, when, why,* and *how* to demonstrate understanding of key details in a text. **Question 3: Literature 2.** Recount stories, including fables and folktales from diverse cultures, and determine their central message, lesson, or moral.

Name _____

## Read the selection. Then answer the questions that follow.

### What Is It?

| | |
|---|---|
| Zhou likes to be near the ocean. He likes to hear the waves. He likes | 15 |
| to put his feet in the sand. He likes to see the birds in the sky. | 31 |
| One day, Zhou saw a little face in the water. The face was dark gray. | 46 |
| The face had black eyes and a long nose like a dog. Zhou saw the face | 62 |
| going up and down in the waves. | 69 |
| "Look! Look!" Zhou said to Mom. | 75 |
| Mom stopped reading her book. | 80 |
| "What is it?" Zhou asked. | 85 |
| "It is a seal," Mom said. "Seals like to swim in the ocean. They look | 100 |
| for fish to eat in the water." | 107 |
| "I like to swim in the ocean too!" Zhou said. | 117 |

**Turn the page.**

**Answer the questions below.**

**1** Which words tell you that this story takes place at the beach?

○ gray, nose, dog, black

● ocean, waves, sand, water

○ feet, sky, Mom, book

**2** Which sentence does not tell about Zhou?

○ He likes to see birds.

● He likes to read.

○ He likes to hear the waves.

**3** How does Zhou feel when he first sees the face in the water?

○ mad

○ sick

● excited

**4** Which sentence tells about Mom?

● She wants Zhou to know about ocean animals.

○ She wishes Zhou would learn to swim.

○ She hopes the seal would go away.

**5** What is this story mostly about?

It is about seeing a new animal in the ocean.

**Common Core State Standards**

Questions 1–4: Literature 1. Ask and answer such questions as *who, what, where, when, why,* and *how* to demonstrate understanding of key details in a text. Question 5: Literature 2. Recount stories, including fables and folktales from diverse cultures, and determine their central message, lesson, or moral.

Name _____

**Read the selection. Then answer the questions that follow.**

### My Great Train Adventure

It was great riding on the train to visit Aunt Rose. I climbed up the | 15

steps and got on the train. I sat in a seat next to the window. The train | 32

began to move slowly. "Here we go, Sam," Dad said. I looked out the | 46

window and watched the trees pass by. | 53

"Tickets, tickets," said a man in a blue jacket and hat. | 64

"Sam, this is the conductor. He takes the tickets for the train ride," | 77

Dad said. | 79

The man smiled and gave me a shiny pin that was shaped like the | 93

train. | 94

A few hours later, I looked out the window and saw a small building | 108

up ahead. As the train got closer, I saw Aunt Rose standing in front of | 123

the building. She was smiling and waving to us. | 132

"This is where we get off," Dad said. | 140

I cannot wait until my next train ride. | 148

**Turn the page.**

**Answer the questions below.**

**1** **Where did the story take place?**

○ on a boat

● on a train

○ on an airplane

**2** **How did Sam feel about riding on the train?**

○ bored

○ afraid

● excited

**3** **What lesson can the reader learn from this story?**

● It is fun to try new things.

○ It is important to stay safe.

○ It is hard to lose old friends.

**4** **How can you tell the conductor was kind?**

# He smiled and gave Sam a pin.

**5** **Do you think Sam's dad is a good father? Tell why or why not.**

# Possible response: I think

# he is a good dad because he

# explains things well to Sam.

**Common Core State Standards**

**Questions 1, 2, 4, 5: Literature 1.** Ask and answer such questions as *who, what, where, when, why,* and *how* to demonstrate understanding of key details in a text. **Literature 3.** Describe how characters in a story respond to major events and challenges. **Question 3: Literature 2.** Recount stories, including fables and folktales from diverse cultures, and determine their central message, lesson, or moral.

**Fresh Reads   Unit 1 Week 1 A**

Name _____

**Read the selection. Then answer the questions that follow.**

**Honey**

| | |
|---|---|
| Bees make honey. They fly from flower to flower. They get nectar | 12 |
| from the flowers to make honey. Then the bees take the nectar back to | 26 |
| their hive. There, they make a lot of honey. People can take honey from | 40 |
| the hive. Be careful! Honey can stick to your hands. Honey tastes good. | 53 |
| It is sweet. Thank you, bees! | 59 |

**Turn the page.**

**Answer the questions below.**

**1** **Where do bees make honey?**

- ○ in the flowers
- ○ in the air
- ● in their hives

**2** **What is the main idea of the selection?**

- ○ Bees like to fly around.
- ○ Honey can stick to your hands.
- ● Bees work hard to make honey.

**3** **What do bees need to make honey?**

- ○ people
- ● flowers
- ○ grass

**4** **Why do you think the author wrote "Thank you, bees!" at the end?**

Possible response: The author likes honey and is happy that the bees make it.

**Common Core State Standards**

**Questions 1, 3: Informational Text 3.** Describe the connection between a series of historical events, scientific ideas or concepts, or steps in technical procedures in a text. **Question 2: Informational Text 1.** Ask and answer such questions as *who, what, where, when, why,* and *how* to demonstrate understanding of key details in a text. **Question 5: Informational Text 6.** Identify the main purpose of a text, including what the author wants to answer, explain, or describe.

**Read the selection. Then answer the questions that follow.**

### The Ballpark

| | |
|---|---:|
| A baseball park is a great place to spend an afternoon. You can go | 14 |
| with your family. You can watch a ball game. | 23 |
| At the game, you can see the baseball teams run on the field. You can | 38 |
| see the players hit the ball. You can cheer for the team you like. You can | 54 |
| jump up and down when your team gets a run. You can clap your hands. | 69 |
| Some people like to eat hot dogs at the ballpark. Some people like to | 83 |
| eat ice cream. Other people do not like to eat anything at all. They just | 98 |
| want to watch the game. | 103 |
| We always have a good time at the ballpark. You can too. | 115 |

**Turn the page.**

**Answer the questions below.**

**1** **What is the main reason most people go to the ballpark?**

- ○ to eat ice cream
- ● to watch a ball game
- ○ to run and play

**2** **The author wrote this selection to**

- ● tell you about something fun to do.
- ○ surprise you.
- ○ teach you how to play a game.

**3** **What is the selection all about?**

- ○ eating hot dogs at the ballpark
- ○ the people who play baseball
- ● things you can do at the ballpark

**4** **Why do people cheer at the ballpark?**

- ○ They want to find their family.
- ● They want to support their team.
- ○ They want to go home.

**5** **Write a new title for "The Ballpark."**

# Possible response: Go, Team, Go!

---

**Common Core State Standards**

**Questions 1, 4: Informational Text 1.** Ask and answer such questions as *who, what, where, when, why,* and *how* to demonstrate understanding of key details in a text. **Question 2: Informational Text 6.** Identify the main purpose of a text, including what the author wants to answer, explain, or describe. **Questions 3, 5: Informational Text 2.** Identify the main topic of a multiparagraph text as well as the focus of specific paragraphs within the text.

Name _____

## Read the selection. Then answer the questions that follow.

### To the Moon and Back

| | |
|---|---|
| Did you ever look into the sky and think what it would be like to | 15 |
| go to the moon? In the summer of 1969, Neil Armstrong became the | 28 |
| first person to walk on the moon. | 35 |
| Armstrong flew to the moon with two other men. But it was | 47 |
| Armstrong who was the first person to walk on the moon. He and Buzz | 61 |
| Aldrin picked up rocks to take back to Earth. The rocks gave scientists | 74 |
| many facts about space. Later, other people flew to the moon too. They | 87 |
| also walked on it and brought rocks back to Earth. | 97 |
| The next time you look at the moon, think about what it must have | 111 |
| been like to be one of these people. | 119 |

**Turn the page.**

**Answer the questions below.**

**1** What detail best supports the idea that there was much to learn from moon rocks?

- ○ Armstrong and Aldrin picked up rocks.
- ● The rocks gave scientists many facts about space.
- ○ Armstrong flew to the moon in 1969.

**2** The author most likely wrote this selection to

- ○ make people laugh at the moon.
- ● tell about real moon walks.
- ○ make people feel sorry for scientists.

**3** What is another good title for the selection?

- ○ The Moon
- ○ Rock Scientists
- ● Armstrong's Walk

**4** What is this selection mainly about?

# The selection is mostly about the first moon walk.

**5** Why is Neil Armstrong important?

# He was the first person to walk on the moon.

**Common Core State Standards**

Questions 1, 3, 4: Informational Text 2. Identify the main topic of a multiparagraph text as well as the focus of specific paragraphs within the text.
Question 2: Informational Text 6. Identify the main purpose of a text, including what the author wants to answer, explain, or describe. Question 5:
Informational Text 1. Ask and answer such questions as *who, what, where, when, why,* and *how* to demonstrate understanding of key details in a text.

**Read the selection. Then answer the questions that follow.**

### The Bluebird

| | |
|---|---:|
| Margaret has a treehouse in her yard. She likes to go there. She likes | 14 |
| to read books by herself. | 19 |
| One day a bluebird flew into the treehouse. | 27 |
| "What are you reading?" the bird asked. | 34 |
| "I'm reading a book about horses," Margaret answered. | 42 |
| "I like horses," the bird said. | 48 |
| "I will read the book to you," Margaret said. | 57 |
| And so she did. | 61 |

**Turn the page.**

**Answer the questions below.**

**1** Where does the story take place?

- ● in a treehouse
- ○ at a park
- ○ on a horse

**2** Which word best tells about Margaret?

- ○ unhappy
- ○ funny
- ● nice

**3** Why does Margaret like the tree house?

- ○ She likes to be near the clouds.
- ● She can go there to read by herself.
- ○ She hears the birds better from there.

**4** Would you like to have Margaret as a good friend? Tell why or why not.

Possible response: She would be a good friend because she is kind to animals.

**Common Core State Standards**

Questions 1–4: **Literature 1.** Ask and answer such questions as *who, what, where, when, why,* and *how* to demonstrate understanding of key details in a text. **Literature 3.** Describe how characters in a story respond to major events and challenges.

## Read the selection. Then answer the questions that follow.

### The Secret Room

| | |
|---|---:|
| Isaac's Uncle Sam lived in the country. He had a big house there. | 13 |
| Isaac and his family lived in the city. They had a small house there. | 27 |
| Sometimes Isaac's family would go to Uncle Sam's house in the | 38 |
| summer. Isaac thought the house was too big. It made a lot of noise. The | 53 |
| house made Isaac feel scared. | 58 |
| One day Isaac heard a noise. He hid under a table by the wall. When | 73 |
| he touched the wall, it opened like a door. Behind the wall was a secret | 88 |
| room. The secret room was full of toys and books. | 98 |
| After that Isaac went to the secret room all the time. Now he feels | 112 |
| happy in the house, not scared. | 118 |

**Turn the page.**

**Answer the questions below.**

**1** **How do you know that Isaac felt scared when he heard the noise?**

● He hid under a table.

○ He touched the wall.

○ He found a secret room.

**2** **Which sentence does not tell about the setting?**

○ "Isaac's Uncle Sam lived in the country."

○ "He had a big house there."

● "One day Isaac heard a noise."

**3** **What happened when Isaac touched the wall by the table?**

○ The wall made a lot of noise.

● The wall opened like a door.

○ The wall made him feel scared.

**4** **Why did Isaac feel better after he found the secret room?**

○ He didn't hear any scary noises.

○ He was able to stay at Uncle Sam's house all year.

● He had fun playing with the books and toys in the room.

**5** **Why do you think Isaac felt scared in Uncle Sam's house?**

## Possible response: The house was big and made noises.

**Common Core State Standards**

Questions 1–5: **Literature 1.** Ask and answer such questions as *who, what, where, when, why,* and *how* to demonstrate understanding of key details in a text. **Literature 3.** Describe how characters in a story respond to major events and challenges.

**Read the selection. Then answer the questions that follow.**

## A Day at the Beach

| | |
|---|---|
| "I've never been to the beach before," said Maria. She had moved | 12 |
| from Nebraska the year before. "We don't have beaches where I used to | 25 |
| live." | 26 |
| "Going to the beach is like going to a carnival," exclaimed Robert, | 38 |
| "because there are many things to do there." | 46 |
| Robert's mother drove Maria and Robert to the beach. When Maria | 57 |
| stepped onto the sand, she jumped. | 63 |
| "The sand feels strange on my bare feet," she said. | 73 |
| Robert taught Maria how to make sand castles. When they were | 84 |
| finished, they decided to walk along the water's edge. Robert saw a | 96 |
| shadow in the water. | 100 |
| "Look, Maria. That is a school of fish," he told her. They watched | 113 |
| until the fish swam out of sight. Then they went into the water. The | 127 |
| waves knocked Maria down, but she didn't mind. | 135 |
| "You were right, Robert," Maria said on their way home. "I love the | 148 |
| beach." | 149 |

**Turn the page.**

**Answer the questions below.**

**1** How did Maria feel when she first stepped onto the sand?

- ○ tired
- ● surprised
- ○ hot

**2** Which sentence best tells about Maria and Robert?

- ○ They lived in the same neighborhood.
- ○ They did not like going to carnivals.
- ● They were good friends.

**3** Which sentence best tells about Maria?

- ● She did not know much about the beach.
- ○ She liked taking walks every day after school.
- ○ She missed her old friends in Nebraska.

**4** What was one new thing that Maria did at the beach?

## Possible response: She made a sand castle.

**5** Would you like to have Robert for a friend? Tell why or why not.

## Possible response: Yes, because he is helpful.

Common Core State Standards

Questions 1–5: **Literature 1.** Ask and answer such questions as *who, what, where, when, why,* and *how* to demonstrate understanding of key details in a text. **Literature 3.** Describe how characters in a story respond to major events and challenges.

**Read the selection. Then answer the questions that follow.**

**Walk or Take the Bus?**

| | |
|---|---|
| When the weather is nice, Pedro walks to school. It takes him | 12 |
| twenty minutes. He walks with his friends. He talks to his friends. He | 25 |
| likes to walk. | 28 |
| When the weather is bad, Pedro takes the bus to school. The bus ride | 42 |
| takes ten minutes. He sits with his friends. He talks to his friends. The | 56 |
| bus is warm and dry. | 61 |

**Turn the page.**

**Answer the questions below.**

**1** What is the selection mostly about?

○ what the bus ride is like

○ how good it feels to walk

● how Pedro gets to school

**2** Which sentence tells what the first paragraph is mostly about?

○ Pedro likes to be with his friends.

○ Pedro rides the bus for ten minutes.

● Pedro walks to school in nice weather.

**3** Which sentence tells what the second paragraph is mostly about?

● Pedro rides the bus to school in bad weather.

○ Pedro walks for twenty minutes to get to school.

○ Pedro and his friends talk as they walk to school.

**4** Sometimes Pedro walks to school and sometimes he takes the bus. How are they the same?

Pedro can talk to his friends when he walks and when he takes the bus.

**Common Core State Standards**

Questions 1–4: **Literature 1.** Ask and answer such questions as *who, what, where, when, why,* and *how* to demonstrate understanding of key details in a text. **Literature 2.** Recount stories, including fables and folktales from diverse cultures, and determine their central message, lesson, or moral.

Name _____

**Read the selection. Then answer the questions that follow.**

### Two Brothers

| | |
|---|---|
| Thalia is happy to have two brothers, Eugene and Alex. They are | 12 |
| different, but they are both good brothers. | 19 |
| Eugene is Thalia's big brother. He is tall and has brown hair. Eugene | 32 |
| likes to sing and play music. He is quiet, and he likes to read books too. | 48 |
| Eugene is very good to his sister. | 55 |
| Alex is Thalia's little brother. He is short and has black hair. Alex | 68 |
| likes games. He likes to run and jump. Alex is always doing something. | 81 |
| He is also very good to his sister. | 89 |
| Sometimes Thalia wants to hear music, so she spends time with | 100 |
| Eugene. Sometimes Thalia wants to play games, so she spends time with | 112 |
| Alex. Thalia is always happy to be with her brothers. | 122 |

**Turn the page.**

**Answer the questions below.**

**1** **What is the selection mostly about?**

● Thalia's brothers

○ Thalia's favorite brother

○ Thalia's brother Alex

**2** **What is the second paragraph mostly about?**

○ what Thalia does with Alex

○ why Thalia is happy

● who Eugene is

**3** **What is the main idea in the third paragraph?**

● Alex is Thalia's younger brother.

○ Eugene is quiet and he likes to read books.

○ Sometimes Thalia wants to play games.

**4** **What is the last paragraph mostly about?**

○ things Eugene enjoys doing

● things Thalia does with her brothers

○ things Alex likes to do

**5** **What is one way that Alex and Eugene are alike?**

## Possible response: They both are good

## to Thalia.

**Common Core State Standards**

Questions 1–5: **Literature 1.** Ask and answer such questions as *who, what, where, when, why,* and *how* to demonstrate understanding of key details in a text. **Literature 2.** Recount stories, including fables and folktales from diverse cultures, and determine their central message, lesson, or moral.

**Read the selection. Then answer the questions that follow.**

### Class Trip

| | |
|---|---|
| When I walked into the museum on our class trip, I could not believe | 14 |
| what I saw. There was a dinosaur skeleton as tall as a house. My teacher | 29 |
| said it lived a long time ago. | 36 |
| I went to the next part of the museum. There were pyramids made of | 50 |
| stone behind large glass windows. There was even a real mummy in a | 63 |
| big box. It looked very old. | 69 |
| The last area was dark. I saw stars painted on the walls. I stared at the | 85 |
| large spaceship hanging in the air. My teacher said it was the first one to | 100 |
| go into space. | 103 |
| On the bus ride back to school, I thought about the spaceship. I want | 117 |
| to come back soon. | 121 |

**Turn the page.**

**Answer the questions below.**

**1** **What is this story mainly about?**

○ looking at a dinosaur

● going to a museum

○ seeing pyramids

**2** **What is another good title for this story?**

○ The Spaceship

● The Museum

○ The Mummy

**3** **Which sentence best supports the idea that the student liked the museum?**

● I want to come back soon.

○ I went to the next part of the museum.

○ The last area was dark.

**4** **How are the dinosaur skeleton and the mummy alike?**

**Possible response: They are both old.**

**5** **What was most likely the student's favorite part of the museum? Explain.**

**I think it was the spaceship. He thought about it later.**

**Common Core State Standards**

Questions 1–3: Literature 2. Recount stories, including fables and folktales from diverse cultures, and determine their central message, lesson, or moral.
Questions 4, 5: Literature 1. Ask and answer such questions as *who, what, where, when, why,* and *how* to demonstrate understanding of key details in a text.

**Read the selection. Then answer the questions that follow.**

### Fun in the Mud

| | |
|---|---|
| Tim wants a frog. He likes frogs. Frogs hop. They jump. | 11 |
| Tim gets a frog. It is a gift from Dad. Tim likes his frog. He names | 27 |
| his frog Bud. | 30 |
| Tim and Bud hop. They jump. They get in some mud. Bud likes the | 44 |
| mud. He digs in it. Tim and Bud have fun in the mud! | 57 |

**Turn the page.**

**Answer the questions below.**

**1** **What kind of pet does Tim want?**

○ a cat

○ a dog

● a frog

**2** **How did Tim get his pet?**

○ He found it in the mud.

● His dad gave it to him.

○ He got it from a friend.

**3** **Where does Tim have fun with his pet?**

○ at the school

● in the mud

○ under the bed

**4** **What does Tim like to do with his new pet?**

# Tim likes to jump and hop and play in the mud with his frog.

**Common Core State Standards**

Questions 1–4: Literature 1. Ask and answer such questions as *who, what, where, when, why,* and *how* to demonstrate understanding of key details in a text.

Name _____

## Read the selection. Then answer the questions that follow.

### What a Mess!

| | |
|---|---:|
| Mom was going to make a cake. Chuck said, "I can help." | 12 |
| Mom got a pan. Chuck got the cake mix. He dropped the box. Some | 26 |
| mix spilled. | 28 |
| Then Chuck got the milk. He dripped some milk on the cake mix. | 41 |
| Mom got an egg. She dropped it. It fell on the cake mix and spilled | 56 |
| milk. It was a mess! | 61 |
| Chuck said, "We did not make a cake." | 69 |
| Mom said, "We made a big mess!" | 76 |
| Chuck got the mop. He mopped up the milk. He mopped up the mix. | 90 |
| He mopped up the egg. He said, "I cleaned up the mess." | 102 |
| Mom said, "Yes, you did. You mopped up the mess. Thank you for | 115 |
| your help." She smiled at Chuck. | 121 |

**Turn the page.**

**Answer the questions below.**

**1** **What does Mom want to do?**

○ take a walk

● make a cake

○ mop the floor

**2** **Where does this story take place?**

● at Chuck's home

○ by Chuck's school

○ in Chuck's yard

**3** **What do Mom and Chuck make?**

○ a toy

○ a cake

● a mess

**4** **Which of these is spilled on the floor?**

○ water

○ juice

● milk

**5** **Why does Mom thank Chuck?**

Possible response: Chuck mopped up

the mess.

**Common Core State Standards**

Questions 1–5: Literature 1. Ask and answer such questions as *who, what, where, when, why,* and *how* to demonstrate understanding of key details in a text.

Name _____

## Read the selection. Then answer the questions that follow.

### The Park on the Hill

| | |
|---|---:|
| "When will Dad be here?" asked Pam. | 7 |
| "He will be back soon, and then we will go have fun," said Mom. | 21 |
| A car honked, and Dad walked in. | 28 |
| "Dad, I am happy you are home," said Pam, and she gave him a | 42 |
| big hug. | 44 |
| Dad said, "I am very glad to be back. It was a long trip, and I missed | 61 |
| you and Mom." | 64 |
| The family went to the park on the hill where there were swings and | 78 |
| a slide. Pam ran up the hill and slid down the slide. Then she got on a | 95 |
| swing and pumped her legs hard. The swing swished back and forth fast. | 108 |
| Mom and Dad sat on a bench. Dad waved at Pam. Everyone had fun | 122 |
| at the park on the hill. | 128 |

**Turn the page.**

**Answer the questions below.**

**1** **Why does Pam hug Dad?**

○ He takes her to the park.

● He comes home from a long trip.

○ He waves when she is on the swing.

**2** **Who honks the car horn?**

○ Mom

● Dad

○ Pam

**3** **Where is the park?**

○ in the woods

○ by a pond

● on a hill

**4** **Why does Pat pump her legs hard when she is on the swing?**

# Pam wants to make the swing go fast.

**5** **Why does Pam want Dad to come home?**

# Pam wants to go have fun at the park with her family.

**Common Core State Standards**

Questions 1–5: Literature 1. Ask and answer such questions as *who, what, where, when, why,* and *how* to demonstrate understanding of key details in a text.

Name _____

**Read the selection. Then answer the questions that follow.**

### Telling Stories

Long ago, people did not have books. They told stories. Some people | 12

were great at telling stories. They used sounds. Sounds made their | 23

stories more interesting. People listening had fun. Hearing stories, they | 33

saw pictures in their minds. They liked that. | 41

People tell stories around the world. And people listen. Stories do | 52

different things. Some stories help people feel good. Others teach things. | 63

The best stories make us laugh. | 69

**Turn the page.**

**Answer the questions below.**

**1** **Which sentence tells an opinion?**

- ○ People tell stories around the world.
- ● The best stories make us laugh.
- ○ Hearing stories, they saw pictures in their minds.

**2** **Why did people tell stories long ago?**

- ○ They did not have music.
- ○ They did not have to work.
- ● They did not have any books.

**3** **According to the passage, what happened when people heard a story?**

- ● They thought of pictures in their minds.
- ○ They wanted to write it down.
- ○ They started making their own sounds.

**4** **Why did people listen to stories?**

**Possible response: The stories were interesting and fun.**

---

**Common Core State Standards**

**Question 1: Informational Text 1.** Ask and answer such questions as *who, what, where, when, why,* and *how* to demonstrate understanding of key details in a text. **Questions 2–4: Informational Text 3.** Describe the connection between a series of historical events, scientific ideas or concepts, or steps in technical procedures in a text.

Name _____

**Read the selection. Then answer the questions that follow.**

## About Birds

Birds are different from other animals in some ways. They have | 11

wings instead of arms. They have feathers instead of hair. Since wings | 23

and feathers help birds move through the air, most birds can fly. | 35

Different kinds of birds eat different types of food. Fruit, plants, | 46

seeds, and bugs are some things birds eat. | 54

Birds make nests for their homes. They lay eggs to have their babies. | 67

Birds sing beautiful songs. The singing makes people very happy. | 77

Some people like to keep birds as pets inside their houses. They like to | 91

hear their birds sing every day. | 97

Other people like to look at birds outside. They count as many | 109

different kinds of birds as they can. Some people feed the birds that | 122

visit their homes. They watch their favorite birds eat right outside their | 134

windows. | 135

**Turn the page.**

**Answer the questions below.**

**1** **Why do birds have wings and feathers?**

○ to help them eat the food

○ to help them build a nest

● to help them fly in the air

**2** **Why do birds lay eggs?**

○ to have food to eat

● to have their babies

○ to make people happy

**3** **For what reason do some people keep birds as pets?**

○ They like to see them fly.

● They like to hear them sing.

○ They like to watch them eat.

**4** **Which sentence from the passage tells an opinion?**

● Birds sing beautiful songs.

○ Birds make nests for their homes.

○ Birds are different from other animals in some ways.

**5** **What happens when people feed the birds that come near their homes?**

They can watch the birds when they are eating.

---

**Common Core State Standards**

Questions 1–3, 5: Informational Text 3. Describe the connection between a series of historical events, scientific ideas or concepts, or steps in technical procedures in a text. **Question 4: Informational Text 1.** Ask and answer such questions as *who, what, where, when, why,* and *how* to demonstrate understanding of key details in a text.

**34** **Fresh Reads   Unit 2 Week 1 OL**

Name _____

## Read the selection. Then answer the questions that follow.

### Life at a Pond

| | |
|---|---|
| A pond is an interesting place to visit. It is filled with fresh water, | 14 |
| which means the water is not salty at all. Some ponds are large, and | 28 |
| others are small. All ponds have something in common. They all have | 40 |
| land around them. | 43 |
| Many different kinds of plants and animals live near ponds. There are | 55 |
| also some plants and animals that actually live in ponds. | 65 |
| Pond mud is a good place for plant roots to grow. Some plants grow | 79 |
| under the water. The water cannot be too deep because the sun has to be | 94 |
| able to reach them. Some plants live on top of the water. Their leaves | 108 |
| float on top of the pond. | 114 |
| Many animals live in or near ponds. They find their food at the | 127 |
| ponds. They can also find water to drink there. | 136 |

**Turn the page.**

**Answer the questions below.**

**1** Which sentence from the passage tells an opinion?

○ They all have land around them.

○ Their leaves float on top of the pond.

● A pond is an interesting place to visit.

**2** What happens when there is no salt in the water?

● The water is fresh.

○ The water is deep.

○ The water is light.

**3** Deep water is bad for growing plants because

○ they cannot float there too long.

● they cannot get enough sunlight.

○ they cannot live in large lakes.

**4** If you jumped into a pond, why would you hear a big splash?

## There would be a splash because ponds are full of water.

**5** Why would places with ponds make good homes for many animals?

## The animals can find plenty of food and water in and near ponds.

Common Core State Standards

**Question 1: Informational Text 1.** Ask and answer such questions as *who, what, where, when, why,* and *how* to demonstrate understanding of key details in a text. **Questions 2–5: Informational Text 3.** Describe the connection between a series of historical events, scientific ideas or concepts, or steps in technical procedures in a text.

## Read the selection. Then answer the questions that follow.

### The Hill and the River

| | |
|---|---|
| The hill said to the river, "You are very long." | 10 |
| "Thank you," said the river. "You are very tall." | 19 |
| "Thank you," said the hill. | 24 |
| "What do you see?" the hill asked. | 31 |
| "I see grass and the sky," said the river. | 40 |
| "What do you see?" the river asked. | 47 |
| "I see grass and the sky," said the hill. | 56 |
| The hill is tall. The river is long. They both see grass and the sky. | 71 |

**Turn the page.**

**Answer the questions below.**

**1** **Why did the author write this story?**

● to tell how the hill and the river were alike and different

○ to tell why the hill and the river were important to people

○ to tell who liked to play near the hill and the river

**2** **How did the author show that the hill and the river were nice to each other?**

○ They said, "You're welcome."

○ They said, "Please."

● They said, "Thank you."

**3** **What is different about the river?**

● It is long.

○ It is blue.

○ It is clean.

**4** **Why did the author have the hill and the river ask each other what they saw?**

## The author wanted to show that they

## both could see the grass and the sky.

**Common Core State Standards**

**Questions 1, 4: Literature 1.** Ask and answer such questions as *who, what, where, when, why,* and *how* to demonstrate understanding of key details in a text. **Questions 2, 3: Literature 3.** Describe how characters in a story respond to major events and challenges.

## Read the selection. Then answer the questions that follow.

### A Pig Knows

| | |
|---|---|
| Jimmy lost his yellow ball. He looked everywhere, but he could not | 12 |
| find the ball by himself. "Can someone help me look for my ball?" A | 26 |
| bird flew by and asked Jimmy what was wrong. "I cannot find my ball." | 40 |
| The bird said, "I'm too busy flying to help you." | 50 |
| Jimmy saw a dog so he asked the dog to help. The dog was too busy | 66 |
| chasing his own ball to help Jimmy. "Who will help me?" Jimmy asked. | 79 |
| Just then a pig came along who said that he would help. "I will use | 94 |
| my nose," said the pig. | 99 |
| The pig put his nose in the grass and snuffled all over the field. He | 114 |
| worked hard trying to find the ball. "Here's your ball!" the pig cried at | 128 |
| last. | 129 |
| "Thanks!" said Jimmy. "You are my new friend. Do you want to play | 142 |
| catch with me?" | 145 |

**Turn the page.**

**Answer the questions below.**

**1** **Why did the author write this story?**

○ to tell how to care for a pet pig

○ to tell what a pig looks like

● to tell how a pig helped a boy

**2** **Why did the author have the pig help Jimmy?**

○ to show that the pig could snuffle

● to show that the pig was friendly

○ to show that the pig can play catch

**3** **How did the author show that the dog was not helpful?**

● by telling that the dog was too busy

○ by having the dog look for the ball

○ by showing that the dog shared his ball

**4** **What is the bird doing when Jimmy asks it for help?**

○ eating

● flying

○ playing

**5** **Why do you think the author made the animals talk in this story?**

Possible response: So they could ask

Jimmy for help.

**Common Core State Standards**

Questions 1–5: Literature 1. Ask and answer such questions as *who, what, where, when, why,* and *how* to demonstrate understanding of key details in a text.

**Read the selection. Then answer the questions that follow.**

### A Helping Hand

| | |
|---|---|
| "Howdy, neighbor," said the rabbit, as he hopped over to the | 11 |
| birdhouse. "My name is Carl." | 16 |
| "My name is Kevin, and I'm pleased to meet you," said the bird. | 29 |
| "You sure have your hands full with this old birdhouse. No one has | 42 |
| lived in it for many, many years," said Carl. | 51 |
| "Well, I am a woodpecker, so I should have it fixed in no time," | 65 |
| Kevin said as he flew inside. For the next several weeks, Kevin | 77 |
| worked day and night. But each time he fixed something, another | 88 |
| thing would break. | 91 |
| One day there was a knock on Kevin's door. Kevin opened it and | 104 |
| saw ten other rabbits with Carl. "We came to assist, neighbor," Carl | 116 |
| said. They worked for a week. When they were finished, the house | 128 |
| was beautiful. As Kevin thanked them, Carl said, "That is what | 139 |
| friends are for." | 142 |

**Turn the page.**

**Answer the questions below.**

**1** How did the author show that the rabbit was friendly?

- ● The rabbit came over to talk with his new neighbor.
- ○ The rabbit brought some food to his new neighbor.
- ○ The rabbit shared his home with his new neighbor.

**2** Why did the author write this story?

- ○ to show what a woodpecker looks like
- ● to teach a lesson about friends
- ○ to tell about a funny thing that happened

**3** What is Kevin?

- ○ a bluebird
- ○ a handy person
- ● a woodpecker

**4** At the beginning of the story, how did the author show that Carl and Kevin did NOT know each other?

They told each other their names.

**5** Why did the author have the rabbits help Kevin fix his house?

So we could know how to be a friend.

**Common Core State Standards**

**Questions 1, 3: Literature 3.** Describe how characters in a story respond to major events and challenges. **Questions 2, 4, 5: Literature 1.** Ask and answer such questions as *who, what, where, when, why,* and *how* to demonstrate understanding of key details in a text.

**Read the selection. Then answer the questions that follow.**

### Apple Cake

| | |
|---|---:|
| Hiroshi and his grandfather are hungry. They want to make an apple | 12 |
| cake. Hiroshi and his grandfather mix the cake. They put it in a pan. | 26 |
| Then they cut up apples. They put the apples on top. Then they cook the | 41 |
| cake. They wait and wait. It smells great. At last, the apple cake is ready. | 56 |
| Hiroshi and his grandfather eat the whole cake. It is very, very good. | 69 |

**Turn the page.**

**Answer the questions below.**

**1** **Why does Hiroshi want to make a cake?**

● He is hungry for something to eat.

○ He likes to surprise his family.

○ He needs to use up some apples.

**2** **Who helps Hiroshi make the cake?**

○ his father

○ his brother

● his grandfather

**3** **What smells great to Hiroshi?**

○ the cake mix

● the baking cake

○ the cut apples

**4** **Why does Hiroshi have to wait?**

# Possible response: He has to wait for the cake to bake all the way through before it can be eaten.

**Common Core State Standards**

**Questions 1–4: Literature 1.** Ask and answer such questions as *who, what, where, when, why,* and *how* to demonstrate understanding of key details in a text. **Literature 3.** Describe how characters in a story respond to major events and challenges.

**Read the selection. Then answer the questions that follow.**

### Helping Shoes

| | |
|---|---|
| One day Juan's mother made him go shopping with her. They went to | 13 |
| buy shoes. Juan hated shopping for shoes. | 20 |
| At the store Juan saw a lot of shoes. First he saw a pair of black | 36 |
| shoes. Then he saw a shiny pair of green shoes. "Can we just get those | 51 |
| and go home?" he asked. | 56 |
| When he wore the green shoes to school, everyone laughed at him. | 68 |
| Suddenly the shoes started walking to the playground! Juan had to go | 80 |
| with the shoes. | 83 |
| When he got to the playground, he saw Lily on the ground. She was | 97 |
| hurt! The shoes took her to the nurse. | 105 |
| "How did you know Lily was hurt?" the nurse asked. | 115 |
| "I did not know," said Juan. "My shoes knew!" | 124 |
| Now Juan loved his green shoes. His shoes took him to people who | 137 |
| needed his help. | 140 |

**Turn the page.**

**Answer the questions below.**

**1** **Juan goes shopping with**

○ his nurse.

○ his friend, Lily.

● his mother.

**2** **Which shoes does Juan buy?**

● the green shoes

○ some black shoes

○ his mother's shoes

**3** **What thing happens first when Juan wears his new shoes to school?**

○ Juan goes back outside to play.

● His classmates all laugh at him.

○ Lily gets hurt on the playground.

**4** **What happens after Juan sees Lily on the ground?**

○ His shoes walk to the playground.

● His shoes take them both to the nurse.

○ His shoes turn bright, shiny green.

**5** **What happens to make Juan go out to the playground?**

His shoes walk him there so he can find
and help Lily.

Common Core State Standards

Questions 1–5: Literature 1. Ask and answer such questions as *who, what, where, when, why,* and *how* to demonstrate understanding of key details in a text.

## Read the selection. Then answer the questions that follow.

### What Is the Answer?

| | |
|---|---|
| Mr. Adams said, "I know a fun game. I will tell you about something, | 14 |
| and you can guess what it is." | 21 |
| Lana said, "That sounds like fun, Dad. My friends Chen and Todd | 33 |
| want to play too." | 37 |
| Mr. Adams said, "This thing has four parts that are thick and strong, | 50 |
| and they all touch the ground." | 56 |
| Todd yelled, "The parts are legs. It's a table!" | 65 |
| Mr. Adams smiled and said, "I have more to tell you about this thing. | 79 |
| It also has a long tube that takes air in and out." | 91 |
| "It's a nose," said Lana. "The thing is some kind of animal." | 103 |
| "This thing has big flaps on two sides. They are thin and feel soft. | 117 |
| They are used to hear," said Mr. Adams. | 125 |
| Chen said, "I know what it is!" | 132 |
| Do you know what it is? | 138 |

**Turn the page.**

**Answer the questions below.**

**1** **Which child belongs to Mr. Adams?**

● Lana

○ Todd

○ Chen

**2** **What does Todd think the thing is?**

○ a horse

○ a chair

● a table

**3** **What is the thing that Mr. Adams tells about?**

○ a cat

○ a monkey

● an elephant

**4** **What makes Lana say that the thing is some kind of animal?**

Lana thinks the long tube is a nose, so it

must be an animal.

**5** **How is Mr. Adams's game played?**

Mr. Adams gives clues about something,

and the children try to guess what it is.

2 Copyright © Pearson Education, Inc., or its affiliates. All Rights Reserved.

**Common Core State Standards**

Questions 1–5: Literature 1. Ask and answer such questions as *who, what, where, when, why,* and *how* to demonstrate understanding of key details in a text.

**Read the selection. Then answer the questions that follow.**

### Honey Bees

| | |
|---|---:|
| Some bees make honey. They use nectar from flowers. Bees work | 11 |
| hard to get nectar. Then they take it to their hive. Hives are where | 25 |
| bees live. | 27 |
|     Where do bees build their hives? Some build them in trees. They | 39 |
| live up high like birds. Birds do not hurt you. Bees can! | 51 |
|     Honey is sweet. Bears like it. People like it too. People learned | 63 |
| about honey. How? They watched bears! | 69 |

**Turn the page.**

**Answer the questions below.**

**1** **What do bees do with the nectar they get?**

● The bees use it to make honey.

○ The bees put it in with flowers.

○ The bees give it to the bears.

**2** **What is the *best* reason that bears like honey?**

○ It is sticky.

● It is sweet.

○ It is thick.

**3** **What happened when people watched bears?**

○ They knew where to build their tree houses.

● They saw how to get honey from beehives.

○ They learned how to use nectar from flowers.

**4** **How are the birds and some bees *alike*?**

Possible response: They both make
their homes up high in the trees.

**Common Core State Standards**

Questions 1–4: Informational Text 1. Ask and answer such questions as *who, what, where, when, why,* and *how* to demonstrate understanding of key details in a text. **Informational Text 3.** Describe the connection between a series of historical events, scientific ideas or concepts, or steps in technical procedures in a text.

**Read the selection. Then answer the questions that follow.**

### Ants

| | |
|---|---|
| Have you ever seen ants? They are fun to watch. They can do many | 14 |
| different things. | 16 |
| Each kind of ant has a certain job. Worker ants are one kind of ant. | 31 |
| They start by finding a place to build a nest. Next, the ants decide what | 46 |
| to use to build the nest. Some ants use a log for the nest. Other ants dig | 63 |
| a nest in the dirt. The worker ants dig lots of tunnels too. They use the | 79 |
| tunnels to go to and from the nest. The worker ants also hunt for food. | 94 |
| Then they bring the food back to the nest for the others. | 106 |
| The queen is another kind of ant. The queen lays the eggs. The | 119 |
| worker ants watch over the eggs. Finally, the babies are born. The | 131 |
| worker ants take care of them. | 137 |

**Turn the page.**

**Answer the questions below.**

**1** **What is the *most likely* reason that ants need to build tunnels?**

○ to hide from their queen

● to go to and from the nest

○ to find where more food is

**2** **Why are some ants called worker ants?**

○ They teach the queen how to work.

○ They work hard to lay the eggs.

● They have a lot of work to do.

**3** **What happens to the eggs when a queen ant lays them?**

● The worker ants will take care of eggs and babies.

○ The worker ants will bury eggs in a log or in the dirt.

○ The worker ants will carry new eggs outside the nest.

**4** **How are all ants *alike*?**

○ They all hunt for food.

● They all have jobs to do.

○ They all lay the eggs.

**5** **What do the worker ants do with the food they find?**

They bring it back to the nest to share with the others.

**Common Core State Standards**

Questions 1–5: **Informational Text 1.** Ask and answer such questions as *who, what, where, when, why,* and *how* to demonstrate understanding of key details in a text. **Informational Text 3.** Describe the connection between a series of historical events, scientific ideas or concepts, or steps in technical procedures in a text.

Name _____

**Read the selection. Then answer the questions that follow.**

## Clean-Up Day at the Beach

| | |
|---|---|
| Mr. Smith took his class on a trip to the beach. When the children | 14 |
| stood on the beach, they saw lots of paper and cans. They saw many | 28 |
| bottles too. It was time to clean up the beach. It was going to be a big | 45 |
| job! They were ready. | 49 |
| The children picked partners to work with. They put on gloves. Then | 61 |
| each pair of children got a trash bag. They walked along the beach, and | 75 |
| they picked up the trash. They stacked the trash bags near a garbage | 88 |
| truck. Mr. Smith threw the heavy bags into the truck. The children | 100 |
| worked hard all morning. When the truck was full of trash bags, the | 113 |
| driver drove away. | 116 |
| The children looked at the beach. Now it was clean. They had done a | 130 |
| good job, and they felt proud. | 136 |

**Turn the page.**

**Answer the questions below.**

**1** What is the *best* reason for the children to wear gloves on Clean-Up Day?

○ to keep their hands warm when it gets cold

● to keep their hands clean when there is trash

○ to keep their hands dry when waves come in

**2** Why is Mr. Smith the person who throws the bags on the truck?

● The bags are too heavy for the children to toss.

○ The children are too tired to lift any more bags.

○ The children have partners, and he does not.

**3** What happens when the garbage truck has been filled up with trash bags?

○ The children add more trash bags.

○ The teacher buries the trash bags.

● The driver takes away the trash bags.

**4** At the end of the story, what has made the children feel proud?

**They worked hard and did a good job cleaning up the beach.**

**5** How does the beach change from the beginning to the end of the story?

**At the beginning, the beach is dirty. At the end, it is clean.**

⎛ **Common Core State Standards**

**Questions 1–3, 5: Literature 1.** Ask and answer such questions as *who, what, where, when, why,* and *how* to demonstrate understanding of key details in a text. **Question 4: Literature 3.** Describe how characters in a story respond to major events and challenges.

**54** **Fresh Reads  Unit 2 Week 4 A**

Name _____

## Read the selection. Then answer the questions that follow.

### Snow

| | |
|---|---|
| My name is Sue. It is snowing. I like the snow. The snow is white. | 15 |
| The snow is wet. The snow is fun. | 23 |
| I run in the white, wet snow. I jump in the white, wet snow. I walk in | 40 |
| the white, wet snow. | 44 |
| At last I go home. I am wet, just like the snow. My mother gives me | 60 |
| hot milk. I am nice and dry now. I am tired too. | 72 |

**Turn the page.**

**Answer the questions below.**

**1** **What tells how the author feels about snow?**

○ The snow is wet.

○ The snow is white.

● The snow is fun.

**2** **How was Sue's milk *different* from the snow?**

○ The milk was brown, but the snow was white.

● The milk was hot, but the snow was cold.

○ The milk was dry, but the snow was wet.

**3** **When Sue got home, how was she *like* the snow?**

○ She was quiet.

○ She was happy.

● She was wet.

**4** **How had Sue changed by the *end* of the story?**

Possible response: Sue had gotten tired from playing in the snow.

2 Copyright © Pearson Education, Inc., or its affiliates. All Rights Reserved.

**Common Core State Standards**

**Questions 1–4: Literature 1.** Ask and answer such questions as *who, what, where, when, why,* and *how* to demonstrate understanding of key details in a text. **Literature 3.** Describe how characters in a story respond to major events and challenges.

Name _____

## Read the selection. Then answer the questions that follow.

### Pets

"Hi, Marco," Lijuan shouts. "Do you want to walk to school with | 12
me?" | 13

"Sure," says Marco. "I just got a new orange fish this weekend. Fish | 26
make the best pets!" | 30

"I think that gerbils make the best pets," says Lijuan. "I can hold my | 44
gerbil and pet him. His brown fur is very soft." | 54

"But can your gerbil swim?" says Marco. | 61

"I don't know. He lives in a cage where he can run around," says | 75
Lijuan. | 76

"I love to watch my fish swim in his tank. He swims all the time," | 91
says Marco. "I like to watch him eat. He swims to the top of the tank | 107
when I put in food." | 112

"Fish sound like fun. Maybe both gerbils and fish are the best pets," | 125
says Lijuan. | 127

"I agree," says Marco. | 131

**Turn the page.**

**Answer the questions below.**

**1** What pet does Marco like *best* at the beginning of the story?

- ● fish
- ○ gerbils
- ○ both fish and gerbils

**2** In what way are Lijuan and Marco *alike*?

- ○ They both have fish.
- ● They both love their pets.
- ○ They both can hold their pets.

**3** Why did the author *probably* write this story?

- ○ to tell people about gerbils and where they live
- ○ to describe two friends walking to their school
- ● to show that different animals can make good pets

**4** How is the gerbil *different* from the fish?

- ● Only the gerbil has fur.
- ○ Only the gerbil can swim.
- ○ Only the gerbil is orange.

**5** In what way are the fish and the gerbil the *same*?

# Possible response: Both of them make

# good pets.

**Common Core State Standards**

**Questions 1–5: Literature 1.** Ask and answer such questions as *who, what, where, when, why,* and *how* to demonstrate understanding of key details in a text. **Literature 3.** Describe how characters in a story respond to major events and challenges.

Name _____

**Read the selection. Then answer the questions that follow.**

### A Good Morning

| | |
|---|---|
| Peter got dressed quickly and went outside this morning. Peter | 10 |
| skipped down the street as he hummed his favorite tune. Peter was an | 23 |
| eight-year-old boy who lived in New York. | 30 |
| "Good morning, Peter," said Mr. Holden, the storekeeper. | 38 |
| "Yes, it is," said Peter. | 43 |
| Then Peter started whistling as he hopped down the street. "Good | 54 |
| morning, Peter," said Officer Carey, the policeman. | 61 |
| "It certainly is," said Peter. | 66 |
| Peter was smiling and giggling as he ran past Miss Brown, the | 78 |
| firefighter. | 79 |
| "Good morning, Peter," she said. | 84 |
| "Yes, it is," said Peter. | 89 |
| Peter dashed up the steps to his grandmother's house and went | 100 |
| inside. She was standing in the kitchen with Peter's birthday present in | 112 |
| her hand. Peter jumped up and gave her a big hug. | 123 |
| "Good morning and happy birthday, Peter," she said. | 131 |
| "Yes, it is," Peter said. | 136 |

**Turn the page.**

**Answer the questions below.**

**1** **Why did the author begin the story with Peter skipping and humming?**

○ to show that Peter was in a hurry

○ to show that Peter liked music

● to show that Peter was happy

**2** **In what way was Peter's greeting for each person the *same*?**

● He agreed with each one that it was a good day.

○ He told each person that today was his birthday.

○ He called each person by his or her correct name.

**3** **In what way were Officer Carey and Miss Brown *alike*?**

○ They both were part of Peter's family.

● They both had jobs that kept people safe.

○ They both lived next to Mr. Holden.

**4** **How was Peter's grandmother *different* from the other people in this story?**

# Possible response: She knew it was his birthday.

**5** **In what way were all the grown-ups in the story the *same*?**

# They all said good morning and called him by name.

2 Copyright © Pearson Education, Inc., or its affiliates. All Rights Reserved.

> **Common Core State Standards**

**Questions 1–5: Literature 1.** Ask and answer such questions as *who, what, where, when, why,* and *how* to demonstrate understanding of key details in a text. **Literature 3.** Describe how characters in a story respond to major events and challenges.

Name _____

**Read the selection. Then answer the questions that follow.**

### Milk

| | |
|---|---:|
| Pedro lives on a farm. His family sells milk. | 9 |
| Pedro's family has many cows. The cows are black and white. They | 21 |
| are very big. They make a lot of noise. They are loud when they are | 36 |
| hungry. Pedro's family feeds the cows. | 42 |
| The milk comes from the cows. Pedro's family puts the milk in | 54 |
| bottles. Then they sell the milk. They work hard. | 63 |
| Sometimes Pedro gets tired of cows. Sometimes Pedro gets tired of | 74 |
| milk. But, mostly, he likes working with his family. | 83 |

**Turn the page.**

**Answer the questions below.**

**1** The author most likely wrote this selection

○ to explain how to feed cows.

○ to make people cry.

● to tell about life on a farm.

**2** What does the author think about Pedro?

● The author thinks Pedro works hard.

○ The author thinks Pedro is lazy.

○ The author thinks Pedro should work less.

**3** What is the big idea behind this story?

○ Cows can make good pets for children.

○ It is noisy when the animals are hungry.

● Working on a family farm is a good life.

**4** Why do you think the author wrote that Pedro gets tired of cows and milk?

## Possible response: The author wants to show that Pedro does not always like to work.

**Common Core State Standards**

Questions 1–3: Literature 1. Ask and answer such questions as *who, what, where, when, why,* and *how* to demonstrate understanding of key details in a text. Literature 2. Recount stories, including fables and folktales from diverse cultures, and determine their central message, lesson, or moral. Question 4: Literature 3. Describe how characters in a story respond to major events and challenges.

**Read the selection. Then answer the questions that follow.**

**Pet Mouse**

| | |
|---|---|
| Mom said, "Sam, a pet mouse is a fun pet to have. But you have to | 16 |
| take good care of him." | 21 |
| Mom and Sam looked at a book about mice. They read that a mouse | 35 |
| needs a warm home. Mom took out the large cage she had bought. Sam | 49 |
| filled the cage with paper to keep his mouse warm and dry. | 61 |
| Next, Mom helped Sam put the water bottle and food bowl in the | 74 |
| mouse's home. "Make sure the water bottle is always full of water. Make | 87 |
| sure the bowl is always full of food," she said. | 97 |
| "Let's build a playground for my mouse so he can run and play!" | 110 |
| Sam said. | 112 |
| Mom put the mouse in his new home. She said, "If you take care of | 127 |
| your mouse, he will be happy and healthy. He is just like you. You need | 142 |
| a warm home, food, and water, and a place to play too!" | 154 |

**Turn the page.**

**Answer the questions below.**

**1** **Why did the author write "Pet Mouse"?**

- ○ to describe a favorite mouse for readers
- ○ to make people laugh at a funny mouse
- ● to tell a story about caring for a mouse

**2** **Which sentence tells the author's main point?**

- ○ Mom and Sam have read a book about mice.
- ● You have to take good care of your pet mouse.
- ○ Make sure that the bottle is always full of water.

**3** **The author writes that Sam and Mom look at a book about mice so that the reader will know they**

- ○ do not know anything about mice.
- ● want to learn about taking care of mice.
- ○ like to read silly stories about mice.

**4** **What lesson can you learn from this story?**

- ● People and animals need many of the same things.
- ○ People who work hard can get a lot of things done.
- ○ People are often afraid to try doing new things.

**5** **What does the author want you to know by the end of the story?**

The author wants me to know how to take care of a pet mouse.

Common Core State Standards

Questions 1, 2, 4, 5: Literature 2. Recount stories, including fables and folktales from diverse cultures, and determine their central message, lesson, or moral.
Question 3: Literature 1. Ask and answer such questions as *who, what, where, when, why,* and *how* to demonstrate understanding of key details in a text.

## Read the selection. Then answer the questions that follow.

### Lost

| | |
|---|---:|
| "Here, Bonzo! Where are you, Bonzo?" Diana called for her dog. | 11 |
| Bonzo had run out of the house when the front door was left open. | 25 |
| Diana and her dad searched all over the neighborhood, but they could | 37 |
| not locate Bonzo. | 40 |
|     That night Diana had an idea. She drew as many pictures of Bonzo as | 54 |
| she could. Then she put the pictures on signs telling about her lost dog. | 68 |
| Diana and her dad posted the signs all over town. She hoped someone | 81 |
| would find Bonzo. Diana anxiously waited by the telephone for six days, | 93 |
| but no one called. She did not give up. | 102 |
|     Finally, on the seventh day, the telephone rang. It was a man who | 115 |
| lived two towns away. He found a dog resembling Bonzo. | 125 |
|     Diana and her dad jumped in the car and went to the man's house. As | 140 |
| soon as Diana exited the car, Bonzo wagged his tail. "Bonzo," exclaimed | 152 |
| Diana, "I knew I would find you!" | 159 |

**Turn the page.**

**Answer the questions below.**

**1** **Why did the author write "Lost"?**

○ to show that dogs can cause problems

● to tell a story about a girl who wouldn't give up

○ to make people laugh about a silly dog

**2** **Why did the author tell the reader about the door being left open?**

○ so the reader would know what Bonzo looked like

● so the reader would know why Bonzo was lost

○ so the reader would know where Bonzo was

**3** **The author wrote that Diana waited by the telephone for six days so that the reader would know**

● how much Diana loved Bonzo.

○ why the telephone finally rang.

○ that Diana had few friends.

**4** **How does the author want you to feel at the end of the story?**

# The author wants me to feel happy that Diana found Bonzo.

**5** **What will Diana and her dad probably do next?**

# They will take Bonzo home.

**Common Core State Standards**

**Questions 1, 2, 4: Literature 2.** Recount stories, including fables and folktales from diverse cultures, and determine their central message, lesson, or moral. **Questions 3, 5: Literature 1.** Ask and answer such questions as *who, what, where, when, why,* and *how* to demonstrate understanding of key details in a text. **Literature 3.** Describe how characters in a story respond to major events and challenges.

Name _____

**Read the selection. Then answer the questions that follow.**

### The Sky

Some people never look up. Some people only look down. But the sky is pretty. Look up at the sky! | 12 | 20

The sky is blue during the day. You will see the sun. You will see birds. Maybe you will see an airplane. The sky is full of things during the day. | 35 | 49 | 51

The sky is black at night. You will see stars. The sky is quiet at night. | 67

Do not look down. Look up! | 73

**Turn the page.**

**Answer the questions below.**

**1** **Why is the sky black at night?**

● because you cannot see the sun

○ because the stars are out

○ because there are birds in the sky

**2** **When would you see a bird?**

● after you look up at the sky

○ before you can see the sky

○ while the sky is dark and quiet

**3** **You can tell that the author**

○ likes the sun more than the stars.

○ thinks airplanes should not be in the sky.

● thinks looking up is more fun than looking down.

**4** **Why is the sky quiet at night?**

Possible response: The sky is quiet at
night because there are not many noisy
things in it.

Common Core State Standards

**Questions 1, 2, 4: Informational Text 1.** Ask and answer such questions as *who, what, where, when, why,* and *how* to demonstrate understanding of key details in a text. **Informational Text 3.** Describe the connection between a series of historical events, scientific ideas or concepts, or steps in technical procedures in a text. **Question 3: Informational Text 8.** Describe how reasons support specific points the author makes in a text.

Name _____

## Read the selection. Then answer the questions that follow.

### Why Leaves Fall in the Fall

| | |
|---|---|
| Sam's grandmother needed help raking leaves. After breakfast he | 9 |
| walked to her house. | 13 |
| "Why don't leaves fall in the spring?" Sam asked. His grandmother | 24 |
| was already raking leaves into piles. | 30 |
| "I'll tell you why," Grandma said. "You see, leaves need water to | 42 |
| make the tree's food. The roots spread out to look for water. In the | 56 |
| spring and summer, they take in water." | 63 |
| Grandma picked up a leaf. "See the little lines running through the | 75 |
| leaf?" she asked. "They are like tiny tubes. They pull up water from the | 89 |
| trunk, which helps the tree to grow." | 96 |
| Grandma added, "By fall a little bit of cork has grown where each | 109 |
| leaf is joined to the tree. The cork stops water from getting to the leaves. | 124 |
| The leaves dry up and fall off. That is why we rake leaves in the fall." | 140 |
| "Thanks, Grandma," Sam said. "Look! We're almost done. I think we | 151 |
| are a great team!" | 155 |

**Turn the page.**

**Answer the questions below.**

**1** **This selection tells you why**

- ○ trees don't grow in the spring.
- ○ roots cannot take up water.
- ● leaves fall in the fall.

**2** **Leaves use water in order to**

- ○ change color.
- ● make the tree's food.
- ○ keep the tree cool.

**3** **What do the "tiny tubes" in a leaf do?**

- ○ stop water from reaching the leaf
- ○ make the leaves fall
- ● pull water from the trunk

**4** **What happens *after* the cork grows in the tree leaves?**

- ● The leaves dry up.
- ○ The leaves turn green.
- ○ The leaves drink water.

**5** **Based on the story, what do you think Grandma's yard is like?**

Possible response: She has many trees
that lose a lot of leaves.

Common Core State Standards

Questions 1–5: Literature 1. Ask and answer such questions as *who, what, where, when, why,* and *how* to demonstrate understanding of key details in a text.

Name _____

## Read the selection. Then answer the questions that follow.

### The Present

| | |
|---|---:|
| Mom and I were shopping. As we passed the art store, Mom stopped | 13 |
| and smiled at a painting of two kittens sleeping next to each other. "Are | 27 |
| you going to buy it?" I asked Mom. "No, Susan," she said. "I do not like | 43 |
| the frame." | 45 |
| Then we passed the pet store. Mom giggled when she saw a kitten | 58 |
| playing with a ball. | 62 |
| The next day was Mom's birthday. Dad asked, "Do you know what | 74 |
| Mom would like for her birthday?" I told him about what happened in | 87 |
| the mall. "Perfect," Dad said. | 92 |
| That night after dinner, Dad gave Mom her present. It was a big | 105 |
| box with holes on the side. When Mom opened the box, a tiny kitten | 119 |
| jumped out onto her lap. "How did you know that is what I wanted?" | 133 |
| Mom asked. | 135 |
| "Just a lucky guess," Dad said. Dad and I laughed. | 145 |

**Turn the page.**

**Answer the questions below.**

**1** How did Susan know that Mom liked the painting?

- ○ Mom told her she liked the painting.
- ● Mom smiled when she saw the painting.
- ○ It was Mom's birthday.

**2** Why did the kitten's box have holes on the side?

- ○ so people could peek at the kitten
- ● so the kitten would have air to breathe
- ○ so the kitten could look outside

**3** How did Mom feel when she saw the kitten playing with the ball?

- ○ sad
- ● amused
- ○ tired

**4** How did Susan know what Mom wanted for her birthday?

**Mom was happy when she saw the painting and kitten.**

**5** What happens *last* in this story?

**After Mom gets the kitten, Susan and Dad laugh about their secret.**

**Common Core State Standards**

Questions 1–4: Literature 1. Ask and answer such questions as *who, what, where, when, why,* and *how* to demonstrate understanding of key details in a text. Question 5: Literature 5. Describe the overall structure of a story, including describing how the beginning introduces the story and the ending concludes the action.

Name _____

## Read the selection. Then answer the questions that follow.

### Trains and Cars

| | |
|---|---|
| Trains and cars can go fast. They go slow too. They carry people. | 13 |
| They also carry things. Cars run on roads. Trains run on two tracks. | 26 |
| Some roads go over tracks. Cars drive over the tracks. | 36 |
| Trains have lights and horns. These say the trains are coming. Cars | 48 |
| must watch out for trains. Cars can stop fast. Trains cannot. | 59 |
| When trains are coming, cars must stop. Cars must stay away from | 71 |
| the tracks. Be safe. Stay back. | 77 |

**Turn the page.**

**Answer the questions below.**

**1** **How are cars and trains the same?**

○ They can only carry people.

● They can go fast or slow.

○ They must stay back from tracks.

**2** **How are trains different from cars?**

● Trains run on two tracks and cars drive on roads.

○ Trains must stop when there are cars coming.

○ Cars sound their horns at the train tracks.

**3** **What can cars do fast that trains have to do slowly?**

○ turn

● stop

○ watch

**4** **Why should a car stay away from the tracks if a train is coming?**

Possible response: The train can hit a car if it is too close to the tracks.

**Common Core State Standards**

**Questions 1–4: Informational Text 1.** Ask and answer such questions as *who, what, where, when, why,* and *how* to demonstrate understanding of key details in a text. **Informational Text 3.** Describe the connection between a series of historical events, scientific ideas or concepts, or steps in technical procedures in a text.

**Read the selection. Then answer the questions that follow.**

### Cheer Up!

| | |
|---|---|
| Hilde was sick with a bad cold. She was in a bad mood because she | 15 |
| hated to be sick. When Hilde's mother asked if she wanted some soup, | 28 |
| Hilde answered, "No!" Hilde was not very nice when she was sick. | 40 |
| Then her friend Arnold visited. Arnold had a cold too, but he was | 53 |
| happy. He did not feel mad when he was sick. | 63 |
| When Hilde's mother asked Arnold if he wanted soup, he answered, | 74 |
| "Yes, please!" Arnold was nice even though he was sick. | 84 |
| Hilde asked Arnold, "How can you be happy when you are sick?" | 96 |
| Arnold answered, "You can be happy any time if you try, because life | 109 |
| is better when you are happy." | 115 |
| After that, Hilde tried to be happy even when she was sick. She also | 129 |
| tried to be nice even when she was not sick. She learned that Arnold was | 144 |
| right. She learned that everything was better when she tried to be happy. | 157 |

**Turn the page.**

**Answer the questions below.**

**1** How are Hilde and Arnold the same?

○ They always feel happy.

○ They are the same age.

● They each have a cold.

**2** In this story, Hilde is *most likely*

● at her home.

○ at the school.

○ at Arnold's house.

**3** How does Arnold act differently from Hilde?

● He is mostly happy and nice.

○ He is mostly mad and mean.

○ He is mostly silly and playful.

**4** What do both Hilde and Arnold know by the end of the story?

○ When you are mean, your friends will not talk to you.

○ When you are sick, some soup makes you feel better.

● When you try to be happy, everything seems better.

**5** How does Hilde change in this story?

At the beginning, she is mean and in a

bad mood. At the end, she tries being

happy, and things are better.

**Common Core State Standards**

**Questions 1–5: Literature 1.** Ask and answer such questions as *who, what, where, when, why,* and *how* to demonstrate understanding of key details in a text. **Literature 3.** Describe how characters in a story respond to major events and challenges.

**Read the selection. Then answer the questions that follow.**

### My New School

| | |
|---|---|
| Today, I started at a new school. My family just moved to a smaller | 14 |
| town. When we lived in the big city, I rode a bus to school. Now we live | 31 |
| so near the school that I can walk there. Mother said, "Pam, you will like | 46 |
| walking." | 47 |
| When it was time to go, I hugged Mother and went outside. I saw | 61 |
| children walking toward the school together. They were having fun with | 72 |
| each other, and they all had many friends. I did not have any friends | 86 |
| here, and I really missed my old friends. My dad had told me I would | 101 |
| make new friends, but I was not so sure. | 110 |
| Suddenly two children started walking with me. The girl said her | 121 |
| name was Kim, and the boy was named Chen. I found out we were in | 136 |
| the same grade. They talked very fast and asked me many things. By the | 150 |
| time we got there, I had two new friends! | 159 |

**Turn the page.**

**Answer the questions below.**

**1** **How is Pam's new school different from her old school?**

● Her new school is close to her house.

○ Her new school is made of bricks.

○ Her new school is in the big city.

**2** **How do Pam, Kim, and Chen all get to school?**

○ They all ride in a bus.

○ They all go in cars.

● They all walk there.

**3** **How is Pam different at the end of the story?**

○ She is scared.

● She is happy.

○ She is lonely.

**4** **How is where Pam used to live different from where she lives now?**

Pam used to live in a big city. Now she lives in a small town.

**5** **How does Pam feel when she sees the other children walking together?**

Pam is sad because she does not have any friends to walk with.

**Common Core State Standards**

Questions 1–5: **Literature 1.** Ask and answer such questions as *who, what, where, when, why,* and *how* to demonstrate understanding of key details in a text. **Literature 3.** Describe how characters in a story respond to major events and challenges.

Name _____

**Read the selection. Then answer the questions that follow.**

### Take Turns

| | |
|---|---|
| Libby and Lucy played ball in front of their house. Libby had a blue | 14 |
| ball. Lucy had a red ball. They were happy. Their friend Henri came | 27 |
| over. | 28 |
| "Do you want to play ball with us?" asked Libby and Lucy. | 40 |
| "I do not have a ball," said Henri. He was sad. | 51 |
| "You can use my ball," said Libby. | 58 |
| "Yes," said Lucy, "We can all take turns." | 66 |
| Now Henri was very happy. "Thank you very much!" said Henri. | 77 |

**Turn the page.**

**Answer the questions below.**

**1** **What happened in the beginning of the story?**

○ Henri felt sad.

○ Lucy and Libby saw Henri.

● Lucy and Libby played ball by themselves.

**2** **What happened in the middle of the story?**

● Henri told the girls that he did not have a ball.

○ Henri thanked the girls for being kind to him.

○ Henri had to go home and look for his ball.

**3** **Why did Henri feel happy at the end of the story?**

○ He found his own ball.

● His friends offered to share a ball with him.

○ He made two new friends.

**4** **What happened to make Henri feel sad?**

Possible response: Henri was sad

because he did not have a ball, and he

thought he would not be able to play.

**Common Core State Standards**

Questions 1–3: **Literature 5.** Describe the overall structure of a story, including describing how the beginning introduces the story and the ending concludes the action. **Question 4: Literature 3.** Describe how characters in a story respond to major events and challenges.

Name _____

## Read the selection. Then answer the questions that follow.

### Boy Potato

| | |
|---|---:|
| Jimmy sat in a chair by the TV all day long. He watched TV and | 15 |
| played video games. He ate potato chips and cookies. Then he ate more | 28 |
| potato chips. | 30 |
| His father often said to Jimmy, "It's a beautiful day! Why don't you | 43 |
| go outside to play?" | 47 |
| But Jimmy liked to sit in a chair by the TV all day long. | 61 |
| His friends often came over and said to Jimmy, "It's a beautiful day! | 74 |
| Why don't you come outside to play?" But Jimmy watched TV and ate | 87 |
| potato chips, and he was happy. | 93 |
| Then one day, Jimmy noticed that he was getting rounder and | 104 |
| rounder. He used to have two eyes, but now he had five or six eyes. | 119 |
| What was happening? Jimmy was turning into a potato right there in | 131 |
| front of the TV! | 135 |
| Then, Jimmy woke up from his dream. He ran outside right away to | 148 |
| run and play with his friends. | 154 |

**Turn the page.**

**Answer the questions below.**

**1** **What happened first in the story?**

○ Jimmy went to sleep and had a dream.

○ Jimmy noticed that he was getting rounder.

● Jimmy watched TV and played video games.

**2** **What did Jimmy do right after he woke up from his dream?**

● He ran outside.

○ He watched more TV.

○ He played video games.

**3** **Why did Jimmy have a bad dream?**

○ He wanted to eat more potato chips.

● He knew that he watched too much TV.

○ He was worried about school.

**4** **What happened to Jimmy *just before* he woke up from his dream?**

○ He played a video game.

● He turned into a potato.

○ His father talked with him.

**5** **What did Jimmy say *after* his friends asked him to come outside to play?**

Possible response: He did not say
anything because he was too busy
watching TV.

> **Common Core State Standards**

Questions 1, 2, 4, 5: Literature 5. Describe the overall structure of a story, including describing how the beginning introduces the story and the ending concludes the action. Question 3: Literature 3. Describe how characters in a story respond to major events and challenges.

**Fresh Reads   Unit 3 Week 4  OL**

## Read the selection. Then answer the questions that follow.

### Jack's First Pottery Class

| | |
|---|---|
| Jack liked to draw. He loved taking art classes in school. Every | 12 |
| holiday he made beautiful drawings as presents for his family. | 22 |
| One day Mom came home very excited. "Jack," Mom said, "guess | 33 |
| what I got for you?" Jack made some guesses, but each time Mom shook | 47 |
| her head no. "I signed you up for a pottery class." | 58 |
| "Pottery?" Jack said. "What is that?" Mom explained that pottery is | 69 |
| when you make things out of clay with your own hands. Jack jumped up | 83 |
| and down. | 85 |
| At the first class Jack met the teacher, Mrs. Slater. She showed Jack | 98 |
| how to put clay on the wheel. The wheel spun around slowly. He put his | 113 |
| hands in water to keep them from sticking to the clay. As he pushed on | 128 |
| the clay, the shape changed. The more he pushed, the more it changed. | 141 |
| When he was finished, Jack had made a clay bowl. He had a huge smile | 156 |
| on his face as he showed Mrs. Slater what he had made. | 168 |
| "When is the next holiday?" Jack wondered. | 175 |

**Turn the page.**

**Answer the questions below.**

**1** Which event happened first?

○ Jack put clay on the wheel.

○ Jack went to his first pottery class.

● Mom had a surprise for Jack.

**2** Why did Jack jump up and down?

○ He was happy that his mother was home.

○ He loved the holidays.

● He was excited about going to the pottery class.

**3** What happened in the middle of the story?

● Jack met Mrs. Slater.

○ Jack made a clay bowl.

○ Jack drew a beautiful picture.

**4** What did Jack already know how to do at the *beginning* of this story?

Jack could already make beautiful drawings.

**5** In the pottery class, what did Jack do next *after* he got his hands wet?

Jack pushed on the clay as the wheel went around. He changed the shape of it.

2 Copyright © Pearson Education, Inc., or its affiliates. All Rights Reserved.

**Common Core State Standards**

Questions 1, 3–5: **Literature 5.** Describe the overall structure of a story, including describing how the beginning introduces the story and the ending concludes the action. **Question 2: Literature 3.** Describe how characters in a story respond to major events and challenges.

Name _____

**Read the selection. Then answer the questions that follow.**

## Be a Teacher!

| | |
|---|---|
| Being a teacher is the best job ever! It is great! First, you must learn | 15 |
| how to teach. Then you can teach others. | 23 |
| Some teachers teach children reading. Reading is the most important | 33 |
| thing to teach. Why? All people need to know how to read. Reading is | 47 |
| fun too. | 49 |
| Teachers also teach about working with numbers. Learning about | 58 |
| numbers is exciting. Once children know their numbers, you can teach | 69 |
| them how to add. | 73 |
| Teaching is the best there is! | 79 |

**Turn the page.**

**Answer the questions below.**

**1** **Which sentence tells an opinion?**

● Being a teacher is the best job ever!

○ First, you must learn how to teach.

○ Once children know their numbers, you can teach them how to add.

**2** **Which sentence tells a fact?**

○ Reading is fun too.

● Some teachers teach children reading.

○ Reading is the most important thing to teach.

**3** **Which sentence tells an opinion?**

● Learning about numbers is exciting.

○ Teachers also teach about working with numbers.

○ Once children know their numbers, you can teach them how to add.

**4** **What do children learn *before* they learn to add?**

Possible response: They learn to count, what numbers mean, and how to read numbers.

2 Copyright © Pearson Education, Inc., or its affiliates. All Rights Reserved.

**Common Core State Standards**

**Questions 1–4: Informational Text 1.** Ask and answer such questions as *who, what, where, when, why,* and *how* to demonstrate understanding of key details in a text.

Name _____

**Read the selection. Then answer the questions that follow.**

### Food

| | |
|---|---:|
| You should eat many different foods each day. Your body needs food. | 12 |
| Food helps you move and think. Food helps your body grow and stay | 25 |
| healthy. | 26 |
| Some foods keep you from feeling tired. You should eat foods like | 38 |
| bread, rice, and cereal so you have energy to run and play. | 50 |
| Fruits and vegetables taste great. They are also fun to eat. They help | 63 |
| keep your body from getting sick. They help get rid of your body's | 76 |
| waste too. | 78 |
| Your body needs foods such as beans, eggs, meat, and fish. You need | 91 |
| milk too. These foods help your body grow, and they help you get better | 105 |
| if you are sick or hurt. | 111 |
| You should stay away from foods with sugar in them. Too much | 123 |
| sugar is not good for your body. | 130 |
| Learning about food is interesting. Read about different foods. Use | 140 |
| what you learn to make good choices about what to eat. Choosing good | 153 |
| foods makes you feel and look good. | 160 |

**Turn the page.**

- - - - - - - - - - - - - - - - - - - - - - - - - - - - - - - - - -

**Answer the questions below.**

**1** **Which sentence tells an opinion?**

○ Your body needs food.

● Learning about food is interesting.

○ They help get rid of your body's waste too.

**2** **Which sentence tells a fact?**

● You need milk too.

○ They are also fun to eat.

○ Read about different foods.

**3** **Which sentence tells an opinion?**

● Fruits and vegetables taste great.

○ Food helps you move and think.

○ Some foods keep you from feeling tired.

**4** **Which sentence tells a fact?**

○ They are also fun to eat.

○ Learning about food is interesting.

● Food helps your body grow and stay healthy.

**5** **What do you do *after* you read about different foods?**

Use what you learn to choose healthy

foods to eat.

Common Core State Standards

**Questions 1–4: Informational Text 1.** Ask and answer such questions as *who, what, where, when, why,* and *how* to demonstrate understanding of key details in a text. **Question 5: Informational Text 3.** Describe the connection between a series of historical events, scientific ideas or concepts, or steps in technical procedures in a text.

Name _____

## Read the selection. Then answer the questions that follow.

### From a Seed to a Fun Food

| | |
|---|---|
| Nothing is better than the smell of popcorn popping. It is a delicious | 13 |
| smell that can make anyone hungry. But how does popcorn turn from a | 26 |
| hard seed into something so good to eat? | 34 |
| The hard shell of a piece of popcorn covers something interesting. | 45 |
| Inside are the parts that would eventually grow into a mature plant if it | 59 |
| were planted. A little bit of water is also inside that shell. | 71 |
| A popcorn seed needs to get very hot to pop. Then the water inside | 85 |
| the shell turns into a gas. The gas requires much more space when it gets | 100 |
| hot. The steam finally pops the seed case wide open. The popcorn seed | 113 |
| turns inside out and looks white. | 119 |
| Making popcorn is a lot of fun. Long ago people played a game with | 133 |
| it. They threw popcorn seeds onto hot rocks in a fire. When the seeds | 147 |
| popped open, popcorn would fly into the air. Even long ago, everyone | 159 |
| loved popcorn. | 161 |

**Turn the page.**

**Answer the questions below.**

**1** **Which sentence tells an opinion?**

● Nothing is better than the smell of popcorn popping.

○ A little bit of water is also inside that shell.

○ The popcorn seed turns inside out and looks white.

**2** **Which sentence tells a fact?**

○ Making popcorn is a lot of fun.

○ The hard shell of a piece of popcorn covers something interesting.

● They threw popcorn seeds onto hot rocks in a fire.

**3** **What happens *after* the water inside the popcorn seed's shell turns to gas?**

● The popcorn shell pops open.

○ The popcorn seed gets very hot.

○ The hard shell covers the soft insides.

**4** **What is the author's opinion about popcorn?**

Popcorn is interesting, and it smells

good when it is popping.

**5** **In your opinion, what is the *best* thing about popcorn?**

Possible response: I think the best thing

is that popcorn looks so cool after it pops.

**Common Core State Standards**

**Questions 1, 2, 5: Informational Text 1.** Ask and answer such questions as *who, what, where, when, why,* and *how* to demonstrate understanding of key details in a text. **Question 3: Informational Text 3.** Describe the connection between a series of historical events, scientific ideas or concepts, or steps in technical procedures in a text. **Question 4: Informational Text 8.** Describe how reasons support specific points the author makes in a text.

Name _____

**Read the selection. Then answer the questions that follow.**

### More Money

| | |
|---|---|
| Tim wanted money to buy a gift for his mother. He did some work | 14 |
| for his dad. Dad gave him money. Tim used it to buy a toy instead. So he | 31 |
| did more work. And Dad gave him more money. Tim still did not have | 45 |
| enough for a present. | 49 |
| Dad said, "Tim, you must save your money. Then you can buy what | 62 |
| you want." | 64 |
| Tim saved his money. He bought a flower in a pretty pot. He gave it | 79 |
| to his mother. She was happy. So was Tim. | 88 |

**Turn the page.**

**Answer the questions below.**

**1** Where does this story take place?

○ at a bank

● at home

○ at school

**2** Why does Dad have Tim do some work?

○ Dad wants to keep Tim very busy.

○ Dad wants Tim to learn new things.

● Dad wants to help Tim earn money.

**3** What is the *most likely* reason Tim buys a flower?

● It is a gift he knows his mother will like.

○ It is what he always gives her as a gift.

○ It is the only gift he is able to find for her.

**4** What lesson does Tim learn in this story?

Possible response: Tim learns how to
save his money so he can buy a gift.

Common Core State Standards

**Questions 1–3: Literature 1.** Ask and answer such questions as *who, what, where, when, why,* and *how* to demonstrate understanding of key details in a text. **Literature 3.** Describe how characters in a story respond to major events and challenges. **Question 4: Literature 2.** Recount stories, including fables and folktales from diverse cultures, and determine their central message, lesson, or moral.

Name _____

**Read the selection. Then answer the questions that follow.**

### A Bear and Her Cub

| | |
|---|---:|
| "It is such a warm, sunny August day," said Barry, a bear cub. | 13 |
| "Yes, it is," said his mother, Bernice, "but not for too much longer." | 26 |
| They came to a berry bush and began to eat. When he was full, Barry | 41 |
| walked away. "You need to eat more," said Bernice. | 50 |
| "Why?" Barry asked. | 53 |
| "Every winter, bears sleep until spring. We need to eat so we will not | 67 |
| be hungry during the winter months," answered Bernice. | 75 |
| The leaves on the trees turned orange and yellow and then fell to | 88 |
| the ground. The two bears ate all day and night. Soon snow began to | 102 |
| fall from the sky. The two bears found a cave, went inside, and fell fast | 117 |
| asleep. | 118 |
| After all the snow had melted, leaves began to appear on the branches | 131 |
| of the trees again. Bernice and Barry came out of their cave. | 143 |
| "Mom, look how big I am," said Barry. He had nearly doubled in | 156 |
| size. "I am hungry." | 160 |
| "Me too," said Bernice, and the two bears left to find some fish. | 173 |

**Turn the page.**

**Answer the questions below.**

**1** **How do you know that it is spring when the bears wake up?**

- ○ The leaves on the trees are yellow and orange.
- ○ The snow has begun to fall from the sky.
- ● The snow is gone and the trees have leaves.

**2** **How old is Barry at the beginning of the story?**

- ○ very old
- ○ a few years old
- ● less than a year old

**3** **According to this story, when do bears eat?**

- ○ fall, winter, and spring
- ● spring, summer, and fall
- ○ winter, spring, and summer

**4** **Which word *best* describes Bernice in this story?**

- ○ silly
- ○ brave
- ● caring

**5** **What surprised Barry when he woke up?**

Possible response: He was surprised he grew so much while he was sleeping.

Common Core State Standards

Questions 1, 3: Literature 1. Ask and answer such questions as *who, what, where, when, why,* and *how* to demonstrate understanding of key details in a text. Questions 2, 4, 5: Literature 3. Describe how characters in a story respond to major events and challenges.

## Read the selection. Then answer the questions that follow.

### Grandpa's Toy Truck

"Oh no!" cried Nancy. "That was my favorite toy." She was upset | 12

because her little brother George had broken her toy truck. Grandpa | 23

came over and tried to fix the truck, but it could not be repaired. | 37

"It is not all George's fault," said Grandpa. "They do not make toys | 50

the way they did when I was a boy." Grandpa explained that the toys | 64

when he was younger were made of stronger materials. For instance, | 75

he had had toy army men that were made out of metal. These days they | 90

were made out of plastic. He had had a doll that was made out of wood. | 106

Grandpa thought his doll was much nicer looking than Nancy's dolls. | 117

"If the toys were made better when you were little," asked Nancy, | 129

"why did they change?" | 133

"Time and money," replied Grandpa. "Today they make toys in half | 144

the time and for less money." | 150

Grandpa went inside. When he returned, he gave Nancy the toy truck | 162

he had kept from when he was her age. "This truck will survive George," | 176

said Grandpa. Nancy thanked him with a hug. | 184

**Turn the page.**

**Answer the questions below.**

**1** **What sort of person is Grandpa?**

● kind

○ foolish

○ greedy

**2** **How did George *most likely* break Nancy's truck?**

○ hiding what he had done

○ putting it away at night

● playing with it one day

**3** **Grandpa *probably* cannot fix the truck because**

● It is poorly made.

○ It needs special tools.

○ It is too small to see.

**4** **According to Grandpa, why are today's toys being made from weaker materials like plastic?**

Toys can be made faster and cheaper with plastic.

**5** **What do you think Grandpa's toy truck is *most likely* made from?**

Grandpa's toy truck is probably made of metal or wood.

2 Copyright © Pearson Education, Inc., or its affiliates. All Rights Reserved.

> **Common Core State Standards**

**Questions 1–3: Literature 3.** Describe how characters in a story respond to major events and challenges. **Questions 4, 5: Literature 1.** Ask and answer such questions as *who, what, where, when, why,* and *how* to demonstrate understanding of key details in a text.

Name _____

**Read the selection. Then answer the questions that follow.**

### Leaf Art

| | |
|---|---:|
| One of the most fun things to do is making pictures from leaves. | 13 |
| First, pick some leaves that are on the ground. Make sure they have | 26 |
| bright colors. Then lay them on a piece of paper. Place another piece of | 40 |
| paper over those leaves. Put a big book on top of everything. What is | 54 |
| next? Let it sit for two days. Take off the book. Your leaves will be dry | 70 |
| and flat. | 72 |
| Last, decide what to make. You can make any picture you want. | 84 |

**Turn the page.**

**Answer the questions below.**

**1** **Which sentence tells an opinion?**

○ Put a big book on top of everything.

○ First, pick some leaves that are on the ground.

● One of the most fun things to do is making pictures from leaves.

**2** **What is the *first* thing you should do to make leaf pictures?**

● Collect some colored leaves.

○ Put leaves on a piece of paper.

○ Let the leaves dry for two days.

**3** **What happens *after* you let the book sit for two days?**

○ The paper is in many pieces.

● The leaves are flat and dry.

○ The book has bright colors.

**4** **What is the *final* step?**

# You must decide what picture you want to make with the leaves.

2 Copyright © Pearson Education, Inc., or its affiliates. All Rights Reserved.

**Common Core State Standards**

**Question 1: Informational Text 1.** Ask and answer such questions as *who, what, where, when, why,* and *how* to demonstrate understanding of key details in a text. **Questions 2–4: Informational Text 3.** Describe the connection between a series of historical events, scientific ideas or concepts, or steps in technical procedures in a text.

Name _____

**Read the selection. Then answer the questions that follow.**

**From Tadpoles to Frogs**

Frogs are interesting animals. Frogs lay eggs in the water. Fish may | 12

eat some of the eggs, but many will become tadpoles. After nine days | 25

tadpoles come out of the eggs. They live in weeds in the water that is not | 41

very deep. They have tails, use gills to breathe in the water, and eat very | 56

small plants. | 58

By the time they are twelve weeks old, tadpoles have changed a lot. | 71

They have grown two back legs and now they have front legs too. Their | 85

lungs are ready to breathe air when they are on land. Soon, tadpoles will | 99

lose their tails. | 102

Now they have become frogs. They live on the land and eat insects | 115

and worms. They breathe with their lungs. They have four legs that are | 128

used for jumping. They also use their legs and feet to swim. They are | 142

great swimmers. Frogs live on the land, but they are still able to swim a | 157

long way in the water. Sometimes they rest in the water, with only their | 171

eyes showing. People have to look very hard to see them. Soon, some of | 185

these frogs will go back to the water to lay eggs. | 196

**Turn the page.**

**Answer the questions below.**

**1** Which of these happens *first* in the selection?

● Frogs lay their eggs.

○ Tadpoles grow legs.

○ Frogs eat the tadpoles.

**2** What happens *right after* the tadpoles come out of their eggs?

● They live around weeds in the water.

○ They lose their tails and their lungs.

○ They grow their back and front legs.

**3** What happens *after* the tadpoles become frogs?

○ They grow more back legs.

● They start living on land.

○ They use their tails to swim.

**4** What must happen *before* frogs can live outside the water?

○ They must wait nine days and grow tails.

● They must have lungs to breathe the air.

○ They must rest with just their eyes showing.

**5** "Tadpoles and frogs eat very different things." What detail in the story proves this statement of fact?

Tadpoles eat small plants, while frogs

eat insects and worms.

**Common Core State Standards**

**Questions 1–4: Informational Text 3.** Describe the connection between a series of historical events, scientific ideas or concepts, or steps in technical procedures in a text. **Question 5: Informational Text 1.** Ask and answer such questions as *who, what, where, when, why,* and *how* to demonstrate understanding of key details in a text.

**100**

**Fresh Reads   Unit 4 Week 2 OL**

Name _____

**Read the selection. Then answer the questions that follow.**

## The Great Gold Hunt

| | |
|---|---:|
| John Sutter moved west in 1839 and bought some land in California. | 12 |
| He built a fort on his land so people would have a safe place to visit and | 29 |
| to live. He also grew food. He sold food to the people who lived near the | 45 |
| fort and to people moving west. Sutter wanted to make a lot of money. | 59 |
| Another man named James Marshall built a saw mill at the fort. He | 72 |
| cut wood for people to use to build fences, houses, and other buildings. | 85 |
| The land around the fort became known as Sutter's Mill. When Marshall | 97 |
| found gold in a nearby river in 1848, Sutter and Marshall wanted to keep | 111 |
| it a secret. They were afraid their workers would leave to look for gold, | 125 |
| and they were right. | 129 |
| It is not easy to keep secrets. One year later, thousands of people | 142 |
| moved west to hunt for gold. The year 1849 was the start of the Gold | 157 |
| Rush. This is why the gold hunters were called Forty-Niners. Soon the | 169 |
| two men had no workers, nothing to sell, and no money. They both died | 183 |
| poor. | 184 |

**Turn the page.**

**Answer the questions below.**

**1** **Which sentence tells an opinion?**

● It is not easy to keep secrets.

○ The land around the fort became known as Sutter's Mill.

○ One year later, thousands of people moved west to hunt for gold.

**2** **Which of the following happened *first* in the selection?**

○ The Gold Rush was started.

○ James Marshall built a saw mill.

● John Sutter bought land in California.

**3** **What happened *after* James Marshall found gold?**

○ John Sutter built a fort to protect people.

● Many people moved out to California.

○ People bought wood from the saw mill.

**4** **What happened to Sutter and Marshall *after* the Gold Rush started?**

They lost everything they had and died poor.

**5** **How do you know that Sutter built his fort *before* Marshall built his mill?**

It says that Marshall built his mill at the fort, so the fort was built first.

Common Core State Standards

Question 1: Informational Text 1. Ask and answer such questions as *who, what, where, when, why,* and *how* to demonstrate understanding of key details in a text. Questions 2–5: Informational Text 3. Describe the connection between a series of historical events, scientific ideas or concepts, or steps in technical procedures in a text.

Name _____

**Read the selection. Then answer the questions that follow.**

### Here Comes the Sun

|  |  |
|---|---|
| The Earth moves around the sun. People can see the sun when it is | 14 |
| on their side of the world. It is dark when the sun is on the world's other | 31 |
| side. | 32 |
| People should be happy to see the sun every day. It does many jobs | 46 |
| for us. The sun gives us light. It shows us how pretty everything is. The | 61 |
| sun also keeps us warm. It helps things live. | 70 |
| The sun looks like a beautiful fireball. But it is a big, hot star. | 84 |
| Learning about the sun is fun! | 90 |

**Turn the page.**

**Answer the questions below.**

**1** Which sentence tells an opinion?

○ People can see the sun when it is on their side of the world.

○ It is dark when the sun is on the world's other side.

● People should be happy to see the sun every day.

**2** Which sentence from the selection tells a fact?

○ Learning about the sun is fun!

○ The sun looks like a beautiful fireball.

● The Earth moves around the sun.

**3** Which of these states an *opinion* of the author?

● The world is a very pretty place.

○ The Earth does many jobs for us.

○ The sun gives people light.

**4** Tell one fact from the selection that tells why the sun is important to people.

Possible response: The sun

keeps us warm.

**Common Core State Standards**

Questions 1–3: Informational Text 1. Ask and answer such questions as *who, what, where, when, why,* and *how* to demonstrate understanding of key details in a text. Question 4: Informational Text 3. Describe the connection between a series of historical events, scientific ideas or concepts, or steps in technical procedures in a text.

Name _____

## Read the selection. Then answer the questions that follow.

### The History of the Airplane

| | |
|---|---:|
| People have dreamed of flying for a long time. First, people went up | 13 |
| into the air in hot air balloons. Then people went up in blimps. Blimps | 27 |
| looked like balloons, but they were dangerous. Gas was used to fill the | 40 |
| blimp. | 41 |
| December 17, 1903, was a cold, windy day in North Carolina. Two | 53 |
| brothers were in North Carolina on a beach. One Wright brother | 64 |
| flew a plane for the first time. Its name was the Flyer. The Flyer flew for | 80 |
| twelve seconds. It did not go very far, but it flew. The beach was a soft | 96 |
| place for the plane to land. | 102 |
| Airplanes have changed a lot since then. In 1939 the first jet plane | 115 |
| flew. It flew for eight minutes. It held only one person, the pilot. The jet | 130 |
| airplane had an engine that pushed the air to make it fly. Over the years, | 145 |
| airplanes began to go faster. They also began to have room for many | 158 |
| people. A passenger airplane first flew faster than the speed of sound | 170 |
| in 1962. | 172 |
| People who fly today should remember the dreamers who made | 182 |
| flying come true for all. | 187 |

**Turn the page.**

**Answer the questions below.**

**1** **Which detail tells why blimps were dangerous?**

● They had been filled with gas.

○ They looked like hot air balloons.

○ They were made before airplanes.

**2** **Which of these is a statement of fact?**

● The Wright brothers flew a plane for the first time.

○ The Wright brothers were the bravest men in North Carolina.

○ Blimps were better than hot air balloons.

**3** **Which of these states an opinion?**

○ Two brothers were in North Carolina on the beach.

○ The jet airplane had an engine that pushed the air to make it fly.

● People who fly today should remember the dreamers.

**4** **What statement of opinion is *most likely* what the author believed?**

○ Flying in airplanes 100 years ago was dangerous and foolish.

● The people who dreamed of flying made the world better.

○ Today's planes should be able to go faster and carry more people.

**5** **Tell a statement of fact about the Wright brothers' airplane. Explain why it is a fact.**

## Possible response: Their plane was named the Flyer. You can look it up and prove if it is true.

**Common Core State Standards**

**Questions 1–4: Informational Text 1.** Ask and answer such questions as *who, what, where, when, why,* and *how* to demonstrate understanding of key details in a text. **Question 5: Informational Text 3.** Describe the connection between a series of historical events, scientific ideas or concepts, or steps in technical procedures in a text.

Name _____

## Read the selection. Then answer the questions that follow.

### Ranch Life

| | |
|---|---|
| Not long ago, there were many large farms called ranches. The best | 12 |
| things about ranching were living on the open land and being around all | 25 |
| the animals. Ranchers owned cattle, sheep, and horses that other people | 36 |
| could buy. Ranching was a great way to make money. | 46 |
| Cattle, horses, and sheep eat grass during the summer. They could be | 58 |
| left alone to eat and drink until they were big enough to sell. However, | 72 |
| in the winter, they had to be fed hay and corn because there was not | 87 |
| enough grass. Ranchers needed cowboys to help them with the animals. | 98 |
| Cowboys enjoyed working with animals. However, they had to go out in | 110 |
| all kinds of weather to feed and water the animals. Caring for the cattle, | 124 |
| horses, and sheep was the hardest part of running a ranch. | 135 |
| Many of today's ranches are much smaller. Today, ranchers use | 145 |
| machines to do a lot of the work. It is sad that our country no longer has | 162 |
| very many large ranches with lots of cowboys. | 170 |

**Turn the page.**

**Answer the questions below.**

**1** **Which of these sentences tells a fact?**

○ Ranching was always a great way to make lots of money.

● Not long ago, there were many large farms called ranches.

○ The best thing about ranching was living on the open land.

**2** **Which of these sentences tells an opinion?**

○ Ranchers owned cattle, sheep, and horses that other people could buy.

○ Cattle, horses, and sheep eat grass during the summer.

● Caring for the animals was the hardest part of running a ranch.

**3** **What detail from the passage supports the idea that ranching is hard work?**

○ They could be left alone to eat and drink until they were big enough to sell.

○ Today, ranchers use machines to do a lot of the work.

● However, they had to go out in all kinds of weather to feed and water the animals.

**4** **What is the author's opinion about cowboys?**

**The author thinks cowboys did a lot of jobs to keep a ranch running.**

**5** **What is the author's opinion about how ranches have changed?**

**Possible response: The author seems sad that ranches have gotten smaller.**

**Common Core State Standards**

Questions 1–2: Informational Text 1. Ask and answer such questions as *who, what, where, when, why,* and *how* to demonstrate understanding of key details in a text. **Questions 3–5: Informational Text 6.** Identify the main purpose of a text, including what the author wants to answer, explain, or describe. **Informational Text 8.** Describe how reasons support specific points the author makes in a text.

## Read the selection. Then answer the questions that follow.

### Never Ate Carrots!

| | |
|---|---|
| Mei Ling's father cooked chicken and carrots for dinner. | 9 |
| "I hate carrots!" said Mei Ling. | 15 |
| "Have you ever tried carrots before?" asked her father. | 24 |
| "No!" said Mei Ling. | 28 |
| "Well, how do you know you do not like them?" asked her father. | 41 |
| "Carrots are no good," said Mei Ling. | 48 |
| "Just try one," said her father, "before you decide." | 57 |
| Mei Ling ate one carrot. | 62 |
| "Hmm," said Mei Ling, "I like carrots a little bit." | 72 |
| "A lesson," said her father. "Before you make up your mind, try it | 85 |
| first. You might like it!" | 90 |

**Turn the page.**

**Answer the questions below.**

**1** **What happened at the beginning of the story?**

○ Mei Ling said she hated vegetables.

● Mei Ling's father cooked a meal.

○ Mei Ling's father told a story.

**2** **Which sentence in the story tells the big idea?**

○ Have you ever had carrots before?

● Before you make up your mind, try it first.

○ Well, how do you know you do not like them?

**3** **How did Mei Ling learn that she liked carrots?**

● She ate one carrot.

○ Her father told her.

○ She ate her dinner.

**4** **Write what happened at the beginning, middle, and end of the story.**

# First, Mei Ling's father cooked chicken and carrots. Then, Mei Ling said she hated carrots. At the end, Mei Ling ate one carrot and liked it.

2 Copyright © Pearson Education, Inc., or its affiliates. All Rights Reserved.

**Common Core State Standards**

Questions 1, 3, 4: **Literature 1.** Ask and answer such questions as *who, what, where, when, why,* and *how* to demonstrate understanding of key details in a text. **Literature 5.** Describe the overall structure of a story, including describing how the beginning introduces the story and the ending concludes the action. **Question 2: Literature 2.** Recount stories, including fables and folktales from diverse cultures, and determine their central message, lesson, or moral.

Name _____

## Read the selection. Then answer the questions that follow.

### In the Garden

| | |
|---|---|
| Dan was a dog who lived near a garden. He protected his garden | 13 |
| by keeping hungry animals away from the vegetables. He did not want | 25 |
| any animals in the garden, but especially he did not want rabbits in his | 39 |
| garden. | 40 |
| One day Dan saw two rabbits come out of a hole in the ground and | 55 |
| hop into the garden. Dan ran as fast as he could, chasing the rabbits. | 69 |
| "Get out of the garden now," he barked sharply. One of the rabbits ran | 83 |
| away, but one just stopped still. "Please do not hurt me," cried the rabbit. | 97 |
| Dan stopped because he saw that this rabbit was only a baby. He was | 111 |
| sorry that he had scared a baby. | 118 |
| Soon the mother rabbit came out of the hole with three more tiny | 131 |
| rabbits. Now Dan knew why these rabbits were in the garden. He made | 144 |
| the rabbits a promise, "If you do not eat too much from the garden, I | 159 |
| will not chase you." | 163 |
| Now when Dan sees the rabbits in his garden, he wags his tail. | 176 |

**Turn the page.**

**Answer the questions below.**

**1** **What is Dan's problem in the story?**

○ He must take care of a flower garden.

○ He does not like rabbit families.

● He must keep animals from eating vegetables.

**2** **Why did Dan run after the rabbits?**

○ The rabbits were playing with Dan.

● The rabbits went into the garden.

○ The baby rabbits were learning to eat.

**3** **Why did the baby rabbit stay still?**

○ It was tired.

● It was afraid.

○ Its mother told it to stop.

**4** **How did Dan feel when he scared the rabbit?**

○ He felt glad.

○ He felt tired.

● He felt bad.

**5** **How did wagging his tail show that Dan had solved his problem?**

It shows that Dan and the rabbits are

friends, and he doesn't have to keep

them out of the garden.

**Common Core State Standards**

Question 1: Literature 5. Describe the overall structure of a story, including describing how the beginning introduces the story and the ending concludes the action.
Questions 2–5: Literature 1. Ask and answer such questions as *who, what, where, when, why,* and *how* to demonstrate understanding of key details in a text.

Name _____

## Read the selection. Then answer the questions that follow.

### Baby Ben

| | |
|---|---|
| Mother brought the baby home. His name was Ben, and Brenda just | 12 |
| stood there and looked at him. Three-year-old Brenda had thought they | 23 |
| would play together. Instead, she had to be very quiet when Ben was | 36 |
| sleeping. Before he came home, she had planned to hold him and dress | 49 |
| him in baby clothes. Now, she thought, "He is too little and he makes | 63 |
| very loud noises when he cries." | 69 |
| Two years later Ben was no longer a baby, and he never stopped | 82 |
| talking. Ben's favorite word was "why." "Why is the sky blue?" "Why | 94 |
| do we have to eat dinner?" "Why do we have to go to bed?" | 108 |
| As soon as Ben was five years old, he was ready for school, just | 122 |
| like Brenda. Ben thought he was special because he could count to six. | 135 |
| Brenda thought he was special too. She promised to take him to school | 148 |
| with her, as long as Ben promised not to hold her hand. As they walked | 163 |
| to school that morning, their mother thought to herself, "I cannot believe | 175 |
| that both of my children are in school now. The next thing I know, | 189 |
| Brenda will be in college and Ben will be graduating from high school." | 202 |

**Turn the page.**

**Answer the questions below.**

**1** **What was Brenda's problem at the beginning of the story?**

● She wanted to play with Ben, but he was too little.

○ The baby clothes she had did not fit Ben.

○ She wanted to take Ben to school, but he could not go.

**2** **What happened in the middle of this story?**

○ Ben and Brenda went to school.

○ Brenda and Ben played together.

● Ben asked questions.

**3** **Why did both children think that Ben was special?**

○ He asked good questions.

○ He was going to school.

● He could count.

**4** **In the first part of the story, what did Brenda learn about a new baby?**

You cannot play with a baby until it gets older.

**5** **What does the story teach about mothers and their children?**

Mothers think children grow up fast.

**Common Core State Standards**

**Questions 1, 2, 4: Literature 5.** Describe the overall structure of a story, including describing how the beginning introduces the story and the ending concludes the action. **Question 3: Literature 1.** Ask and answer such questions as *who, what, where, when, why,* and *how* to demonstrate understanding of key details in a text. **Literature 3.** Describe how characters in a story respond to major events and challenges. **Question 5: Literature 2.** Recount stories, including fables and folktales from diverse cultures, and determine their central message, lesson, or moral.

## Read the selection. Then answer the questions that follow.

### The Swing

| | |
|---|---|
| Dad and Mark were outside. The car had a flat tire. Dad was | 13 |
| changing it. Mark was raking the grass. "What will you do with the old | 27 |
| tire?" asked Mark. | 30 |
| Dad said, "It has a hole in it, so it is no good anymore." | 44 |
| Mark thought for a minute. Then he said, "Sis wants a swing. Could | 57 |
| we use that old tire to make one?" | 65 |
| "That is a good idea!" said Dad. "We have some long, strong rope." | 78 |
| Mark said, "I know the best tree for a swing. Sis will be so happy!" | 93 |

**Turn the page.**

**Answer the questions below.**

**1** **What is the big idea behind this story?**

○ You can help others by saying kind words.

● One person's trash is another person's prize.

○ There is always more than one way to solve a problem.

**2** **What is Dad's problem in the story?**

○ The rope is missing.

● The car has a flat tire.

○ The grass needs raking.

**3** **What happens in the middle of the story?**

○ Mark uses a long rope.

○ Mark is raking the grass.

● Mark tells about his idea.

**4** **What is this story *mostly* about?**

**Possible response: Mark thinks of a way to get a swing for his sister.**

Common Core State Standards

**Questions 1, 4: Literature 2.** Recount stories, including fables and folktales from diverse cultures, and determine their central message, lesson, or moral.
**Questions 2, 3: Literature 5.** Describe the overall structure of a story, including describing how the beginning introduces the story and the ending concludes the action.

Name _____

**Read the selection. Then answer the questions that follow.**

### Joe's Baby Sister

| | |
|---|---|
| "Joe, please watch the baby for me," said Mom. "I have to go make | 14 |
| dinner now, but I will be right in the next room. Call me if you need | 30 |
| me." | 31 |
| Joe stopped reading his book and looked over at his sister. The | 43 |
| baby was on a soft blanket on the floor. She was reaching for a stuffed | 58 |
| elephant, but it was a little too far away. Joe watched the baby try and | 73 |
| try to get the toy. She did not give up. | 83 |
| Joe thought about what his father said. He said that sometimes you | 95 |
| have to keep working hard to get what you want. Then Joe thought about | 109 |
| how he would feel if he were the baby and never able to reach the toy. | 125 |
| Joe got up and moved the elephant a little closer to the baby. Now the | 140 |
| baby might reach the toy if she tried hard. Joe was glad he had helped | 155 |
| when his little sister grabbed the elephant and laughed. Joe went back to | 168 |
| his reading, and the baby played with her toy. | 177 |

**Turn the page.**

- - - - - - - - - - - - - - - - - - - - - - - - - - - - - - - - - - - -

**Answer the questions below.**

**1** **What is the big idea behind this story?**

○ Life is full of little surprises.

○ Everyone is afraid of something.

● Work hard to get what you want.

**2** **What problem does Joe's baby sister have?**

○ She cannot stand up alone.

○ She cannot see her mother.

● She cannot reach her toy.

**3** **Who helps solve the baby's problem?**

● Joe

○ Dad

○ Mom

**4** **What happens at the end of the story?**

○ Mom goes to the next room to make dinner.

○ Joe thinks about what Dad told him.

● The baby plays with her stuffed elephant.

**5** **What is this story *mostly* about?**

Possible response: The story is about how a boy helps his baby sister.

Common Core State Standards

**Questions 1, 5: Literature 2.** Recount stories, including fables and folktales from diverse cultures, and determine their central message, lesson, or moral.
**Questions 2–4: Literature 5.** Describe the overall structure of a story, including describing how the beginning introduces the story and the ending concludes the action.

Name _____

## Read the selection. Then answer the questions that follow.

### The Helper

| | |
|---|---|
| Sara thought about all the things her mother did around the house. | 12 |
| Mom washed the family's dishes and clothes, and she kept the house | 24 |
| neat and clean. She cooked the meals and made sure the family always | 37 |
| had good food to eat. She also always made time to help Sara with her | 52 |
| homework, even when she was tired. Sara thought her mom was the best | 65 |
| mother in the world! | 69 |
| Sara picked up her room every day, but she realized she lived in the | 83 |
| rest of the house too. She felt it was time to do more things to help her | 100 |
| mom around the house. Sara thought of some things she could do each | 113 |
| day and some things she could do once a week. | 123 |
| Sara didn't tell her mother ahead of time what she was going to do. | 137 |
| She just started doing more things around the house. She put toys away, | 150 |
| and she helped make dinner. She felt very proud when one night Mom | 163 |
| said, "I want to thank my surprise helper. Sara, you have made my job | 177 |
| much easier!" | 179 |

**Turn the page.**

- - - - - - - - - - - - - - - - - - - - - - - - - - - - - - - - - - - - - - - -

**Answer the questions below.**

**1** **What is this story _mostly_ about?**

● A girl finds ways to help her mother.

○ A girl and her mother have fun cooking.

○ A girl sees all the work her mother does.

**2** **What happens at the beginning of the story?**

○ Sara makes dinner and cleans up any messes right away.

○ Sara feels proud because her mom liked having her help.

● Sara thinks about some of the things her mom does around the house.

**3** **What happens at the end of the story?**

● Mom thanks Sara for her help.

○ Mom washes the family's clothes.

○ Mom helps Sara do her homework.

**4** **Tell one job around the house that Sara already does before the story begins.**

## Possible response: She already cleans her room.

**5** **What is the big idea behind this story?**

## Possible response: Helping others makes you feel good.

**Common Core State Standards**

Questions 1, 5: Literature 2. Recount stories, including fables and folktales from diverse cultures, and determine their central message, lesson, or moral. Questions 2, 3: Literature 5. Describe the overall structure of a story, including describing how the beginning introduces the story and the ending concludes the action. Question 4: Literature 1. Ask and answer such questions as *who, what, where, when, why,* and *how* to demonstrate understanding of key details in a text.

**Read the selection. Then answer the questions that follow.**

### Chinese New Year

| | |
|---|---:|
| People have parties when a new year begins. Old things become part | 12 |
| of the past. It is time for new things. It is the best holiday! | 26 |
| The New Year is the most important holiday for Chinese people. | 37 |
| Their parties last for two weeks! They spend time with the family. They | 50 |
| visit their friends. They thank farmers for the food they grow. Day seven | 63 |
| is every person's birthday! | 67 |
| The last day is the most special. People carry lights into the streets. | 80 |
| They have fun together. Chinese people have the best way to start a new | 94 |
| year. | 95 |

**Turn the page.**

**Answer the questions below.**

**1** **Which sentence tells an opinion?**

○ They thank farmers for the food they grow.

○ People have parties when a new year begins.

● It is the best holiday!

**2** **Which sentence tells a fact?**

● People carry lights into the streets.

○ The last day is the most special.

○ Chinese people have the best way to start a new year.

**3** **Why did the author write this story?**

○ to make readers smile and laugh

● to give information about a holiday

○ to tell people they should go to China

**4** **Tell a statement of fact from the selection. Explain why it is a statement of fact instead of an opinion.**

**Possible response: "Their parties last for two weeks." You could look it up in a book about China.**

2 Copyright © Pearson Education, Inc., or its affiliates. All Rights Reserved.

/ **Common Core State Standards** \

**Questions 1, 2, 4: Informational Text 1.** Ask and answer such questions as *who, what, where, when, why,* and *how* to demonstrate understanding of key details in a text. **Question 3: Informational Text 6.** Identify the main purpose of a text, including what the author wants to answer, explain, or describe. **Informational Text 8.** Describe how reasons support specific points the author makes in a text.

**Read the selection. Then answer the questions that follow.**

## Why We Sleep

Do you ever wonder why you have to sleep every night? Sleep is | 13

important for your body and your mind, and dreaming is fun. Staying | 25

up late is exciting. But after moving around all day, your body becomes | 38

tired. Sometimes napping will help your body feel better for a while. For | 51

your body to stay healthy, however, you need to rest all night. | 63

Sleep helps you stay well and grow. You need sleep to do well in | 77

school and to play hard. You can help give your body the rest it needs by | 93

getting about ten hours of sleep every night. | 101

Going to bed at the same time each night helps your body learn when | 115

it is time to rest. Sometimes children stay up too late watching television | 128

or playing computer games. This is a terrible thing to do. Turn off the | 142

television and the computer before bedtime to help you sleep better. | 153

While some children like to read or play games in bed, that is not a | 168

good idea. You should only use your bed for sleeping. That way, your | 181

body learns that it is time to sleep when you are in bed. | 194

**Turn the page.**

**Answer the questions below.**

**1** **Which sentence tells an opinion?**

● Staying up late is exciting.

○ Sleep helps you stay well and grow.

○ Your body becomes tired after moving all day.

**2** **You should only use your bed for sleeping.**

**What fact *best* supports this statement of opinion?**

● It is how your body learns that it is time to fall asleep.

○ Reading or playing games in bed is never a good idea.

○ Turning off the computer is the best way to sleep better.

**3** **Which sentence tells an opinion?**

○ You need sleep to do well in school.

● This is a terrible thing to do.

○ Your body can learn that it is time to sleep.

**4** **Why did the author write this passage?**

○ to tell about a funny dream

● to explain why sleep is important

○ to make readers fall asleep

**5** **Tell a statement of fact from the passage. Explain why it is a statement of fact.**

**Possible response: "Sleep helps you stay well and grow." You can ask a doctor.**

**Common Core State Standards**

**Questions 1, 2, 3, 5: Informational Text 1.** Ask and answer such questions as *who, what, where, when, why,* and *how* to demonstrate understanding of key details in a text. **Question 4: Informational Text 6.** Identify the main purpose of a text, including what the author wants to answer, explain, or describe. **Informational Text 8.** Describe how reasons support specific points the author makes in a text.

**Read the selection. Then answer the questions that follow.**

**Water on the Move**

Water is all around us. You may not always see it, but it is certainly there. Water moves from the ground to the air and back to the ground. All the water that there will ever be on Earth is already here. It is hard to imagine that there is not any new water.

Some water appears to stay on the ground in places such as lakes, rivers, and oceans. Sunshine warms up the water until the water changes to a gas. This is called water vapor, and it rises into the air. You cannot see water vapor, but it is floating above the Earth. When water vapor cools off, it forms clouds of different shapes and sizes. Finding cloud pictures in the sky is a great way to spend time. Clouds are very interesting to observe.

Cooler water is heavier than water vapor. When the water in a cloud gets too heavy to float, it falls to the ground as rain or snow. That is how water moves from the air to the ground. It is best when water comes back as snow. All children love to play outside in water that has turned to snow.

| | 15 |
| 29 |
| 46 |
| 54 |
| 67 |
| 78 |
| 94 |
| 107 |
| 119 |
| 134 |
| 137 |
| 150 |
| 167 |
| 181 |
| 195 |
| 197 |

**Turn the page.**

**Answer the questions below.**

**1** **Which sentence states an opinion?**

○ Sunshine warms up the water until the water changes to a gas.

○ Cooler water is heavier than water vapor.

● It is hard to imagine that there is not any new water.

**2** **Which sentence is a statement of fact?**

○ Clouds are very interesting to observe.

○ It is best when water comes back as snow.

● You cannot see water vapor, but it is floating above the Earth.

**3** **Which sentence tells an opinion?**

○ This is called water vapor, and it rises into the air.

● Finding cloud pictures is a great way to spend time.

○ Water moves from the ground to the air and back to the ground.

**4** **Give one opinion from the selection. Tell one fact that supports that opinion.**

"Finding cloud pictures is a great way to spend time." Clouds have many shapes.

**5** **Why did the author _most likely_ write this passage?**

It was written to explain how water moves between the ground and the sky.

Common Core State Standards

Questions 1–4: Informational Text 1. Ask and answer such questions as *who, what, where, when, why,* and *how* to demonstrate understanding of key details in a text. Question 5: Informational Text 6. Identify the main purpose of a text, including what the author wants to answer, explain, or describe. Informational Text 8. Describe how reasons support specific points the author makes in a text.

**Read the selection. Then answer the questions that follow.**

### Growing Plants

| | |
|---|---:|
| Mother gave Ann a pack of seeds for her birthday. Dad gave her a | 14 |
| little red pot. Ann filled the pot with soil. She put three seeds in the soil. | 30 |
| Then she added some water. She placed the pot in the window. That way | 44 |
| it could get sun. | 48 |
| Ann looked in the pot every day. She gave it water if it was dry. | 63 |
| One day, Ann looked in it. She saw something green. The green thing | 76 |
| was pushing out of the soil. The next day, two more came up. Ann was | 91 |
| growing three plants! | 94 |

**Turn the page.**

**Answer the questions below.**

**1** **Which detail from the passage tells about something that plants need to grow?**

○ Dad gave her a little red pot.

● She gave it water if it was dry.

○ She saw something green.

**2** **Why does Ann place the little pot in the window?**

● to give it light from the sun

○ to give it soil from the yard

○ to give it water from the sink

**3** **What happens when the seeds start to grow?**

○ The brown soil splashes on the window.

● The little plants push up through the soil.

○ The warm sun breaks the little red pot.

**4** **For what reason does Ann look in the pot every day?**

Possible response: She wants to see if
the seeds are growing yet.

/ **Common Core State Standards**

**Questions 1–3: Literature 1.** Ask and answer such questions as *who, what, where, when, why,* and *how* to demonstrate understanding of key details in a text.
**Question 4: Literature 3.** Describe how characters in a story respond to major events and challenges.

**Read the selection. Then answer the questions that follow.**

### Nuts for the Winter

A chipmunk named Melvin lived in Vermont with three other | 10

chipmunks in a hole of an oak tree. On a beautiful summer day, Melvin | 24

gathered nuts that fell from the trees onto the ground. He brought nuts to | 38

his hole in the oak tree because he knew he needed food for the winter. | 53

In another tree lived a squirrel named Steve. All Steve wanted to do | 66

was play. One day Steve saw Melvin picking up nuts. "Melvin, let's play | 79

hide-and-seek," said Steve. | 82

"I don't have time. I must get more nuts," said Melvin. "You should | 95

collect nuts too," said the other chipmunks, but Steve ignored them and | 107

kept playing. | 109

When winter came, snow covered the ground. Melvin looked out | 119

from his tree and saw Steve digging in the snow searching for food. The | 133

other chipmunks went, "Tsk, tsk, tsk, Steve. We warned you." Steve | 144

looked so sad and hungry that Melvin felt sorry for him. He decided | 157

to invite Steve over for a meal. | 164

"Thank you, Melvin. I learned a lesson," said Steve. "I will pay you | 177

back in the spring." Melvin smiled and ate some more. | 187

**Turn the page.**

**Answer the questions below.**

**1** During what time of year does Steve learn an important lesson?

- ○ spring
- ○ summer
- ● winter

**2** For what reason does Melvin bring nuts to his oak tree?

- ○ The nuts will be gifts for his friends.
- ● The nuts will be his food for the winter.
- ○ The nuts will make his house look pretty.

**3** What causes Melvin to feel sorry for Steve?

- ● Melvin sees that Steve is sad and hungry.
- ○ Melvin knows that Steve wants to play.
- ○ Melvin wishes Steve would come for lunch.

**4** What is the effect of the snow when Steve digs for nuts?

- ○ He is able to collect many nuts.
- ● He has trouble finding any nuts.
- ○ He get nuts to share with his friends.

**5** What happens to make Steve thankful at the end of the story?

Steve is thankful that Melvin was willing to share with him.

2  Copyright © Pearson Education, Inc., or its affiliates. All Rights Reserved.

**Common Core State Standards**

Questions 1, 2, 4: Literature 1. Ask and answer such questions as *who, what, where, when, why,* and *how* to demonstrate understanding of key details in a text. Questions 3, 5: Literature 3. Describe how characters in a story respond to major events and challenges.

Name _____

**Read the selection. Then answer the questions that follow.**

### Changing a Bully

| | |
|---|---:|
| Roger, who is not very nice, lives in North Dakota. In fact, Roger is | 14 |
| just plain mean to other kids. All the children in his third-grade class are | 28 |
| afraid of him because he is a bully. | 36 |
| One Saturday morning, two friends, Brian and Manuel, went to the | 47 |
| park to play catch. Suddenly Brian said, "Oh, no, here comes Roger." | 59 |
| The two boys pretended they did not see Roger, but it didn't work. Roger | 73 |
| approached Brian, snatched the ball away, and tossed it into the pond. | 85 |
| Manuel asked Roger, "Why are you so mean?" | 93 |
| For a few seconds, Roger acted as though he would not answer. Then | 106 |
| he said sadly, "No one ever wants to play with me." | 117 |
| "Would you like to play catch with us?" asked Brian. | 127 |
| A big smile appeared on Roger's face. He reached into the pond | 139 |
| and pulled out the ball. The three boys played all morning. Then Roger | 152 |
| thanked the boys, waved good-bye, and walked away, whistling. | 161 |
| Brian scratched his head and looked at Manuel. "I guess a little | 173 |
| kindness goes a long way," said Manuel. | 180 |

**Turn the page.**

- - - - - - - - - - - - - - - - - - - - - - - - - - - - - - - - - - - - - - - -

**Answer the questions below.**

**1** Why are the other children afraid of Roger?

○ Roger is very quiet.

○ Roger is new in town.

● Roger is mean to them.

**2** Roger *most likely* throws the ball in the pond

● to keep it away from Brian and Manuel.

○ to show Brian and Manuel that it will sink.

○ to toss it farther than Brian or Manuel can.

**3** What causes Roger to get the ball out of the pond?

○ Roger wants to run away from there.

○ Roger wants to take it home with him.

● Roger wants to play some catch.

**4** For what reason does Brian ask Roger to play catch?

## Possible response: Brian feels sorry for Roger and wants to be kind to him.

**5** What do Brian and Manuel do when they first see Roger in the park?

## They pretend not to see him.

Common Core State Standards

**Questions 1–5: Literature 1.** Ask and answer such questions as *who, what, where, when, why,* and *how* to demonstrate understanding of key details in a text.
**Literature 3.** Describe how characters in a story respond to major events and challenges.

**Read the selection. Then answer the questions that follow.**

### Captain

| | |
|---|---|
| Tomorrow was the day the teacher would say who was going to be | 13 |
| captain of the baseball team. Mario wanted to be captain. He wanted | 25 |
| to be captain so much that he thought about it every minute. He had | 39 |
| dreamed about being captain. He had talked about being captain. | 49 |
| The next day, the teacher said, "Bill will be captain this year." | 61 |
| Mario was very, very sad, but he liked Bill. Bill would be a good | 75 |
| captain. Mario decided that he would play hard. He would be the best | 88 |
| player on the team. That would make up for not being the captain. | 101 |

**Turn the page.**

**Answer the questions below.**

**1** **What happened at the beginning of the story?**

● Mario wanted to be the captain of the team.

○ Mario wanted to be the best player on the team.

○ Mario was sad that Bill was made captain.

**2** **At the end, why did Mario want to be the best player on the team?**

○ to show Bill that he was better

● to feel better for not being captain

○ to show that he should be captain next year

**3** **What is the big idea of this story?**

○ If you want something badly enough, you will get it.

○ If you want something, you will always be disappointed.

● If you do not get what you want, make the best of it.

**4** **Use your own words to retell the story.**

Mario wanted to be the team captain.

The teacher picked Bill. So, Mario

decided to be the best player.

**Common Core State Standards**

Questions 1, 2: Literature 5. Describe the overall structure of a story, including describing how the beginning introduces the story and the ending concludes the action. Question 3: Literature 1. Ask and answer such questions as *who*, *what*, *where*, *when*, *why*, and *how* to demonstrate understanding of key details in a text. Question 4: Literature 2. Recount stories, including fables and folktales from diverse cultures, and determine their central message, lesson, or moral.

Name _____

**Read the selection. Then answer the questions that follow.**

### José Learns to Fish

| | |
|---|---|
| José and his grandfather lived in Texas. One day they decided to | 12 |
| go fishing in the lake. Grandfather was a good fisherman. He had won | 25 |
| many awards for catching big fish. | 31 |
| First, Grandfather showed José how to put bait on the hook. He used | 44 |
| a worm. Next, he showed José how to cast the hook far into the lake | 59 |
| where the fish were. Finally, he showed José how to make the bait move | 73 |
| in the water to attract fish. José was fishing in no time. | 85 |
| "I got one!" screamed José as his fishing rod bent like a candy cane. | 99 |
| "Pull your rod easy so you don't lose him," said Grandfather. José | 111 |
| slowly pulled the fish in. Grandfather scooped up the fish with a net. | 124 |
| "That's a nice little fish." | 129 |
| After Grandfather took the fish off the hook, he threw it back into the | 143 |
| water. "What did you do that for?" asked José with a confused look on | 157 |
| his face. | 159 |
| "Now the fish will be able to grow bigger. It is called catch and | 173 |
| release," said Grandfather. | 176 |
| "I want to catch a released fish," said José. Grandfather laughed. | 187 |

**Turn the page.**

**Answer the questions below.**

**1** How did José know his Grandfather was a good fisherman?

○ He liked to eat fish.

● He won awards for catching fish.

○ He fished in the lake.

**2** What was the first thing José needed to learn in order to fish?

○ how to move the bait in the water

○ how to cast the bait into the water

● how to put the worm on the hook

**3** Why did José's fishing rod bend?

○ It would attract fish in the water.

○ Grandfather used the net.

● The fish was pulling the rod.

**4** Why did Grandfather throw the fish back into the lake?

○ The fish could not be eaten.

● The fish could grow bigger.

○ The lake would have more fish.

**5** What did José mean when he said he wanted to catch a "released fish"?

He wanted to catch a bigger fish that he could keep.

2 Copyright © Pearson Education, Inc., or its affiliates. All Rights Reserved.

**Common Core State Standards**

**Questions 1, 3, 4, 5: Literature 1.** Ask and answer such questions as *who, what, where, when, why,* and *how* to demonstrate understanding of key details in a text. **Question 2: Literature 5.** Describe the overall structure of a story, including describing how the beginning introduces the story and the ending concludes the action.

## Read the selection. Then answer the questions that follow.

### Sarah's First Day at School

| | |
|---|---|
| Sarah's family had just moved to California. It was her first day at | 13 |
| her new school. | 16 |
| The morning bell sounded, telling students it was time to go to class. | 29 |
| Sarah was lost. She felt as though she were walking in circles. She could | 43 |
| not find her classroom. | 47 |
| "You are new here, and you look like you need some help," said a | 61 |
| brown-eyed boy. "My name is Jack." He held out his hand to Sarah. | 74 |
| "Hello, I'm Sarah," she said as she shook Jack's hand. "I think I am | 88 |
| totally lost. I am looking for my third-grade science class." | 98 |
| "Hey, I'm in that class. I'll walk with you," said Jack, and the two | 112 |
| new friends went down a hall to their class. At recess Jack gave Sarah | 126 |
| a tour of the school. During the tour, Jack told Sarah about the town and | 141 |
| where the park and the library were located. | 149 |
| At the end of the day, Sarah waved good-bye to Jack. "You were a | 163 |
| lifesaver today," she said. | 167 |
| "Don't mention it," said Jack. "Tomorrow I'll tell you where to buy | 179 |
| the best ice cream cone in town." | 186 |
| Sarah smiled. | 188 |

**Turn the page.**

**Answer the questions below.**

**1** **What problem does Sarah have?**

○ She does not know how to make friends.

○ She misses her school in Utah.

● She does not know her way around a new school.

**2** **How did Jack know Sarah needed help?**

○ Sarah was in the wrong building.

● Jack knew that she was a new student.

○ The morning bell had rung.

**3** **What did Jack tell Sarah at the end of the story?**

○ his name

● where the park and library were

○ where the science class was

**4** **Why did Sarah call Jack a "lifesaver"?**

Jack helped Sarah at her new school.

**5** **Why does Sarah smile when Jack tells her, "Tomorrow I'll tell you where to buy the best ice cream cone in town"?**

She knows she has a new friend.

**Common Core State Standards**

**Questions 1–3: Literature 5.** Describe the overall structure of a story, including describing how the beginning introduces the story and the ending concludes the action. **Questions 4, 5: Literature 1.** Ask and answer such questions as *who, what, where, when, why,* and *how* to demonstrate understanding of key details in a text.

**Read the selection. Then answer the questions that follow.**

### Fighting Fires

| | |
|---|---|
| Todd sat in the library reading a book. He liked to read about fire | 14 |
| fighters. He wanted to be a fire fighter when he grew up. He thought | 28 |
| it would be exciting. He would drive the fire truck. He would blow its | 42 |
| horn. | 43 |
| Todd thought fire fighters were brave. They helped people stay safe. | 54 |
| Just then, he heard a loud sound. He saw people looking out the | 67 |
| window. He ran to the window too. He saw a fire truck go by. He did not | 84 |
| know where they went. He did know they would help people. | 95 |

**Turn the page.**

**Answer the questions below.**

**1** **Where does this story take place?**

○ a house

● a library

○ a school

**2** **What is the big idea behind this story?**

○ People run when they can hear loud sounds.

○ Reading is an important skill for you to learn.

● Fighting fires is an exciting way to help people.

**3** **Todd *most likely* reads a book about fire fighters because**

○ he cannot find any sports story he wants.

● he wants to fight fires when he grows up.

○ he knows he must learn how to put out fires.

**4** **How does Todd *probably* feel when he hears the fire truck? Explain why.**

# Possible response: He is probably excited because he wants to drive a fire truck when he grows up.

**Common Core State Standards**

**Question 1: Literature 1.** Ask and answer such questions as *who, what, where, when, why,* and *how* to demonstrate understanding of key details in a text.
**Literature 5.** Describe the overall structure of a story, including describing how the beginning introduces the story and the ending concludes the action.
**Question 2: Literature 2.** Recount stories, including fables and folktales from diverse cultures, and determine their central message, lesson, or moral.
**Questions 3, 4: Literature 3.** Describe how characters in a story respond to major events and challenges.

## Read the selection. Then answer the questions that follow.

### The Fishing Trip

John and Guy lived in Maine. They were best friends and did | 12

everything together. One day they went to the beach to go fishing. They | 25

loved to fish more than anything else. It was a very hot day, so John | 40

grabbed a bottle of juice out of his bag. After he drank the juice, John | 55

tossed the empty bottle into the ocean. | 62

"What did you do that for?" asked Guy. He frowned at John. | 74

"There are no garbage cans anywhere, so there was no other place to | 87

put the empty bottle. Besides, everyone does that," said John. | 97

"Everyone does NOT do that. Throwing things into the ocean is | 108

littering. Fish live in the water and throwing things into the water can | 121

harm them," said Guy. "How would you like it if I threw bottles in your | 136

house?" | 137

John thought about what Guy had said. He used his fishing rod to get | 151

the bottle out of the water and put it in his bag. Guy, smiling at John, | 167

said, "You have made some fish very happy." | 175

**Turn the page.**

**Answer the questions below.**

**1** **What is the big idea behind this story?**

- ● Do not litter.
- ○ Do not waste time.
- ○ Do not talk too much.

**2** **Where does this story take place?**

- ○ at a park
- ○ in a forest
- ● on a beach

**3** **What makes Guy disapprove of his best friend?**

- ● Guy doesn't like John's littering.
- ○ John tells Guy that he doesn't really like fishing.
- ○ Guy learns that John is moving away.

**4** **Which of the following *best* describes what kind of person Guy is?**

- ○ guilty
- ● responsible
- ○ easy going

**5** **How does Guy teach John a lesson about throwing things away?**

Guy compares the fish's home to John's home.

**Common Core State Standards**

**Questions 1, 5: Literature 2.** Recount stories, including fables and folktales from diverse cultures, and determine their central message, lesson, or moral. **Question 2: Literature 5.** Describe the overall structure of a story, including describing how the beginning introduces the story and the ending concludes the action. **Questions 3, 4: Literature 3.** Describe how characters in a story respond to major events and challenges.

Name _____

**Read the selection. Then answer the questions that follow.**

### Sandra Faces the Music

| | |
|---|---:|
| CRASH! The lamp in the living room slid to the floor and smashed | 13 |
| into pieces. Sandra had known better than to throw a football, or any | 26 |
| ball, in the house. | 30 |
| "I am in big trouble," she thought. She swept up all the broken pieces | 44 |
| and threw them in the trash can outside. She did not want her mother to | 59 |
| find out about the lamp and punish her. "I don't want to get grounded. I | 74 |
| want to go to see the high school parade tomorrow." | 84 |
| That evening, before her mother went into the living room, Sandra | 95 |
| sneaked in and turned on the ceiling light. With a strange look on her face, | 110 |
| Mother sat down to read the newspaper. "How was your day?" she asked. | 123 |
| "I didn't do anything," Sandra said quickly. | 130 |
| Mother had a puzzled look on her face. "What happened, Sandra?" | 141 |
| she asked. | 143 |
| Tears filled Sandra's eyes as she told Mother about the broken lamp. | 155 |
| "You are grounded for one week," said Mother, "because you threw | 166 |
| a ball in the house and broke the lamp. But you also need time to think | 182 |
| about how you tried to hide your mistake." | 192 |
| "I have learned two lessons," thought Sandra. "Follow the rules, and | 201 |
| be honest. If I had done that, I would be going to the parade." | 215 |

**Turn the page.**

**Answer the questions below.**

**1** Why does Sandra take the pieces of the lamp outside?

- ○ She must clean up any mess that she makes.
- ● She does not want to get into any trouble.
- ○ She has to sweep the living room each day.

**2** Which word *best* describes Sandra's actions in this story?

- ○ brave
- ● foolish
- ○ jealous

**3** What is the big idea behind this story?

- ○ It is hard to fool your mother.
- ○ It is fun to try out new things.
- ● It is important to be honest.

**4** How does Sandra's mother feel when she learns what Sandra has done?

Sandra's mother is probably disappointed that Sandra broke the rules.

**5** How does Sandra feel at the end of the story?

Sandra is sorry that she broke the lamp and wasn't honest about it.

**Common Core State Standards**

**Question 1: Literature 1.** Ask and answer such questions as *who, what, where, when, why,* and *how* to demonstrate understanding of key details in a text.
**Questions 2, 4, 5: Literature 3.** Describe how characters in a story respond to major events and challenges. **Question 3: Literature 2.** Recount stories, including fables and folktales from diverse cultures, and determine their central message, lesson, or moral.

**Read the selection. Then answer the questions that follow.**

### How Bear Lost His Tail

| | |
|---|---|
| Long ago, Bear had a fine, long tail. He said he had the prettiest tail | 15 |
| of all. This made Fox angry. So Fox played a trick on Bear. | 28 |
| Fox knew Bear liked eating fish. Fox went to the frozen pond. He | 41 |
| took some fish with him. Fox sat down beside a hole in the ice. Bear | 56 |
| walked over. Bear was impressed by Fox's fish. Fox told Bear he used | 69 |
| his tail to catch them. | 74 |
| Bear put his tail into the hole. Then Bear's tail froze into the ice. | 88 |
| When he stood, his tail broke off. Now Bear has a short tail. | 101 |

**Turn the page.**

**Answer the questions below.**

**1** **Which word *best* describes Fox?**

- ○ silly
- ○ brave
- ● clever

**2** **What is the *first* paragraph mostly about?**

- ○ Bear's tail turns to ice and falls off.
- ● Fox gets angry about Bear's bragging.
- ○ Fox tells Bear how to catch fish.

**3** **What is the *last* paragraph mostly about?**

- ○ Fox pretends he has caught some fish at the pond.
- ● Bear loses his tail when he puts it in a hole in the ice.
- ○ Bear tells everyone that his tail is the prettiest one.

**4** **What is another good title for this story?**

Possible response: Bear
Learns a Lesson

**Common Core State Standards**

**Question 1: Literature 3.** Describe how characters in a story respond to major events and challenges. **Questions 2, 3: Literature 1.** Ask and answer such questions as *who, what, where, when, why,* and *how* to demonstrate understanding of key details in a text. **Literature 5.** Describe the overall structure of a story, including describing how the beginning introduces the story and the ending concludes the action. **Question 4: Literature 2.** Recount stories, including fables and folktales from diverse cultures, and determine their central message, lesson, or moral.

**Read the selection. Then answer the questions that follow.**

### Sam and the Dragon

| | |
|---|---|
| A very mean dragon lived in a faraway forest. The fiery dragon | 12 |
| frightened away anyone who tried to enter the forest, except Sam. | 23 |
| One day at King Rocco's castle, Sam saw and fell in love with the | 37 |
| king's daughter, Princess Jessica. "I want to ask your daughter to marry | 49 |
| me," Sam told the king. | 54 |
| "I will allow you to ask her if you bring me a dragon's tooth," said | 69 |
| the king. Sam agreed and set off into the forest. When the dragon | 82 |
| spotted Sam, he shot fire and smoke from his nose and almost burned | 95 |
| Sam. Sam jumped behind a rock. He peered around the rock at the | 108 |
| dragon, surprised to see that the dragon was crying. | 117 |
| "What's the matter?" asked Sam. | 122 |
| "I have a splinter in my hind foot." | 130 |
| Sam pulled the splinter out of the dragon's back foot. | 140 |
| "Oh, thanks," said the dragon. "Can I do something for you?" | 151 |
| Sam asked the dragon for one of his teeth. He pulled an old tooth out | 166 |
| of his pocket and gave it to Sam. | 174 |
| Sam returned to the castle with the tooth. That night he asked | 186 |
| Princess Jessica to marry him. | 191 |

**Turn the page.**

**Answer the questions below.**

**1** **Where does this story take place?**

● in a forest

○ at the beach

○ on a mountain

**2** **What is the *beginning* of the story mostly about?**

○ Sam hides behind a large pile of rocks.

● Sam falls in love with the king's daughter.

○ Sam brings a dragon's tooth to the castle.

**3** **What is the *middle* of the story mostly about?**

● The dragon tries to scare Sam.

○ The dragon gives Sam a tooth.

○ The dragon is mean to the king.

**4** **What is the *end* of the story mostly about?**

○ Sam meets Princess Jessica at the castle.

● Sam and the dragon help each other out.

○ The dragon shoots fire and smoke at Sam.

**5** **What is the main idea of this story?**

If you are kind to others, they may be kind to you.

**Common Core State Standards**

**Questions 1–4: Literature 5.** Describe the overall structure of a story, including describing how the beginning introduces the story and the ending concludes the action. **Question 5: Literature 1.** Ask and answer such questions as *who, what, where, when, why,* and *how* to demonstrate understanding of key details in a text. **Literature 2.** Recount stories, including fables and folktales from diverse cultures, and determine their central message, lesson, or moral.

Name _____

**Read the selection. Then answer the questions that follow.**

### When Mouse Meets Snake

| | |
|---|---:|
| Manny the mouse lived in the forest. One day he came upon a snake | 14 |
| under a tree that had fallen. He turned to run away, but the snake said, | 29 |
| "Please help me. This tree fell on top of me and I can't move." | 43 |
| "If I set you free, you will eat me," said Manny. | 54 |
| "I promise I will not eat you," said the snake. | 64 |
| Manny felt sorry for the snake, so he made a hole in the tree with his | 80 |
| teeth, and the snake slid out. | 86 |
| "Thank you," said the snake. "My name is Suzie. If you ever need | 99 |
| help, just call me. I will help you." Then Suzie slid out of sight. | 113 |
| The next day Manny was eating cheese in Mr. Smith's shed. | 124 |
| Suddenly he was caught in a mouse trap. Manny's tail was stuck, and | 137 |
| he could not get free. He didn't know what to do. Then he remembered | 151 |
| what the snake had told him, so Manny yelled, "SSUUZZZIEEEEE!" | 161 |
| Very soon, Suzie slid into the shed and freed Manny from the trap. | 174 |
| "Thanks," said Manny. "You saved my life." | 181 |
| "Now we're even, friend," said Suzie, and she slid away. | 191 |

**Turn the page.**

**Answer the questions below.**

**1** **What is the beginning of the story _mostly_ about?**

○ Manny chews a hole in the tree.

● Suzie is caught under a fallen tree.

○ Suzie helps Manny get out of a trap.

**2** **What _best_ describes both Suzie and Manny?**

○ hungry and lonely

○ angry and mean

● kind and helpful

**3** **What _best_ supports the idea that mice and snakes are usually enemies?**

○ "Thank you," said the snake.

● "If I set you free, you will eat me," said Manny.

○ Then Suzie slid out of sight.

**4** **What would be another good title for this story?**

**Kindness Builds Friendships**

**5** **What is the big idea of this story?**

**Treat others with trust and kindness,**

**and they may be nice in return.**

**Common Core State Standards**

**Question 1: Literature 5.** Describe the overall structure of a story, including describing how the beginning introduces the story and the ending concludes the action. **Question 2: Literature 3.** Describe how characters in a story respond to major events and challenges. **Question 3: Literature 1.** Ask and answer such questions as _who, what, where, when, why,_ and _how_ to demonstrate understanding of key details in a text. **Questions 4–5: Literature 2.** Recount stories, including fables and folktales from diverse cultures, and determine their central message, lesson, or moral.

**Read the selection. Then answer the questions that follow.**

### Casey's Pets

| | |
|---|---|
| Casey has a cat, a dog, and a fish. She likes her cat best. Her cat is | 17 |
| pretty. Her cat has soft fur. Her cat's fur is black and white. Her cat | 32 |
| cleans herself a lot. Her cat sits on her bed. | 42 |
| Casey thinks her fish is boring. It just swims. She cannot pet it. | 55 |
| Casey thinks her dog is smelly. He runs around the yard a lot. He gets | 70 |
| dirty. His fur always falls out. Casey thinks her cat is smarter than her | 84 |
| dog. She does not want another dog. Dogs are too much trouble. | 96 |

**Turn the page.**

**Answer the questions below.**

**1** **Which pet does Casey like best?**

○ her fish

● her cat

○ her dog

**2** **What does Casey *most likely* believe about owning a cat?**

○ Cats should always live outdoors.

○ Living with a cat means lots of trouble.

● Taking good care of a cat is easy.

**3** **How are Casey's cat and dog *alike*?**

● They both have a lot of fur.

○ They both are clean.

○ They both are very smart.

**4** **Write two ways that Casey's cat and dog are *different*.**

# Possible response: Casey's dog is not very clean, but her cat is clean. Her cat is smart, but her dog is not smart.

┌─ **Common Core State Standards**

**Questions 1, 2: Literature 3.** Describe how characters in a story respond to major events and challenges. **Questions 3, 4: Literature 1.** Ask and answer such questions as *who, what, where, when, why,* and *how* to demonstrate understanding of key details in a text.

Name _____

## Read the selection. Then answer the questions that follow.

### Happy Birthday

Today my friend Eva is having her birthday party at school. She | 12

is from Denmark. Eva told us that in Denmark, a flag is put outside a | 27

window in the house of someone having a birthday. She also told us that | 41

presents are placed around a sleeping child's bed so they will be seen as | 55

soon as the child wakes up. That sounds like fun. | 65

Our teacher told us that birthday parties started a long time ago. | 77

She said that they were first celebrated in Europe. People would bring | 89

presents to friends and family to bring them good thoughts and wishes. | 101

My friend Yara is from Brazil. She said that in Brazil the birthday | 114

children get a pull on the ear for each year they have been alive. The | 129

birthday person also gives the first piece of cake to his or her mother, | 143

father, or most special friend. | 148

I told my class that in China, where I come from, children receive | 161

gifts of money from our parents. Then for lunch we have noodles to | 174

wish the birthday child a long life. | 181

It is a lot of fun learning how my friends from different countries | 194

celebrate their birthdays. The cake Eva brought in for her birthday was | 206

delicious. | 207

**Turn the page.**

## Answer the questions below.

**1** What is *alike* about birthdays in Denmark and China?

- ○ flags
- ○ noodles
- ● presents

**2** How are birthday children *different* in Brazil?

- ○ They feed their friends.
- ● They have their ears pulled.
- ○ They have birthday cakes.

**3** In Denmark, why are flags put in the windows?

- ○ to thank people for birthday presents
- ● to let people know it is someone's birthday
- ○ to give as a present to the birthday person

**4** What food is the *same* at birthday parties in both Brazil and the United States?

- ● cake
- ○ apples
- ○ noodles

**5** What is the same about birthday parties everywhere?

Possible response: People enjoy having birthday parties.

**Common Core State Standards**

Questions 1, 2, 4, 5: Informational Text 3. Describe the connection between a series of historical events, scientific ideas or concepts, or steps in technical procedures in a text. Question 3: Informational Text 1. Ask and answer such questions as *who, what, where, when, why,* and *how* to demonstrate understanding of key details in a text.

**Read the selection. Then answer the questions that follow.**

### Autumn Fun

| | |
|---|---|
| "Grandpa! Grandpa!" Anita yelled as she ran to up to a man with a | 14 |
| short gray beard and white hair. | 20 |
| "Anita, you picked a great day to visit," said Grandpa. "Today is the | 33 |
| autumn festival. The whole town will be there." | 41 |
| "Is that like the winter festival we went to last year?" asked Anita. "I | 55 |
| really liked that. I drank hot chocolate, went ice skating, and we all made | 69 |
| snowmen in the park. However, my favorite part was the snowball fight." | 81 |
| "At the autumn festival we celebrate the good harvest of the crops we | 94 |
| grew all year long," said Grandpa with a smile. "There is dancing in the | 108 |
| barn and plenty of food for everyone. I can almost taste the apple cider | 122 |
| now! Then we bob for apples." | 128 |
| "Bob for apples! What's that?" asked Anita. | 135 |
| "A very large tub is filled with water. Then apples are put into the | 149 |
| water. People try to pick up an apple out of the water with their mouth | 164 |
| without using their hands." | 168 |
| "That sounds hard to do, and wet too," said Anita, laughing. "I think | 181 |
| it will be fun. You know, Grandpa, I think I can almost taste the apple | 196 |
| cider too." | 198 |
| Grandpa laughed. | 200 |

**Turn the page.**

**Answer the questions below.**

**1** **How are Grandpa and Anita *alike*?**

- ○ They have never seen any snow.
- ● They enjoy going to the festivals.
- ○ They are good at bobbing for apples.

**2** **How is the autumn festival *different* from the winter festival?**

- ○ The whole town takes part in it.
- ● It celebrates the good harvest.
- ○ It only happens once each year.

**3** ***Both* festivals in this story celebrate**

- ● seasons.
- ○ families.
- ○ birthdays.

**4** **How are dancing and ice skating *alike*?**

They are both fun and part of the festivals.

**5** **How does Anita feel about visiting her grandfather?**

Anita is excited to visit her grandfather.

Common Core State Standards

**Questions 1–4: Literature 1.** Ask and answer such questions as *who, what, where, when, why,* and *how* to demonstrate understanding of key details in a text. **Question 5: Literature 3.** Describe how characters in a story respond to major events and challenges.

**Read the selection. Then answer the questions that follow.**

## About Bats

| | |
|---|---|
| Bats are strange animals. Why? In some ways, they are like birds. | 12 |
| Both bats and birds can fly. They have wings. They are strong to move | 26 |
| through the air. | 29 |
| In other ways, bats are different from birds. Bats have hair instead of | 42 |
| feathers. Bats are born live. They do not come from eggs. | 53 |
| Bats live in warm places. But they build their homes in cool spots | 66 |
| like caves. Some bats live with just a few other bats. Others live together | 80 |
| with many other bats. They stay in their homes during the day. Bats | 93 |
| come out to eat at night. | 99 |

**Turn the page.**

**Answer the questions below.**

**1** Which sentence tells an opinion?

- ○ Both bats and birds can fly.
- ● Bats are strange animals.
- ○ Bats have hair instead of feathers.

**2** The author tells you about birds to

- ● show that bats are bird-like animals.
- ○ show how birds and bats help people.
- ○ show why birds are better than bats.

**3** The author tells when bats eat to explain why bats

- ○ have wings.
- ● fly at night.
- ○ live in caves.

**4** Why did the author *most likely* write this selection?

**Possible response: The author wanted to tell you things about bats.**

---

**Common Core State Standards**

**Question 1: Informational Text 1.** Ask and answer such questions as *who, what, where, when, why,* and *how* to demonstrate understanding of key details in a text. **Questions 2–4: Informational Text 6.** Identify the main purpose of a text, including what the author wants to answer, explain, or describe. **Informational Text 8.** Describe how reasons support specific points the author makes in a text.

**Read the selection. Then answer the questions that follow.**

### Farming Fish

| | |
|---|---|
| Is there a kind of fish that you like to eat? Maybe it comes in a can, | 17 |
| or maybe it is fresh. The oceans are full of fish, and fish is food for | 33 |
| many animals and people. You may know that many fish come from the | 46 |
| ocean. You may not know that some of the fish you eat are grown on a | 62 |
| farm, rather than being caught in the wild by fishers. | 72 |
| Fish caught wild in the ocean taste better than fish grown on farms. | 85 |
| But it is hard to catch enough fish in the sea. Today, a lot of fish are | 102 |
| grown on fish farms. These farms have big cages that hold lots of fish. | 116 |
| People or machines feed the fish until they are ready for people to eat. | 130 |
| The fish cages give fish a safe place to live and grow. Some people | 144 |
| think that fish farms are a good way to make sure people have enough | 158 |
| food. Other people think the farms are bad because they hold the fish in | 172 |
| a small place and they cannot swim free. | 180 |
| As long as people want to eat fish, other people will find ways to get | 195 |
| them the food they like. | 200 |

**Turn the page.**

**Answer the questions below.**

**1** The author starts the story with a question so that you think about

● your own experience.

○ people living everywhere.

○ why fish cost so much.

**2** Which sentence tells an opinion?

○ These farms have big cages that hold lots of fish.

● Fish caught wild in the ocean taste better than fish grown on farms.

○ People or machines feed the fish until they are ready for people to eat.

**3** Why did the author write the *second* paragraph?

○ to tell about different kinds of fish people eat

● to tell about the fish being raised on fish farms

○ to tell how fish are served in different countries

**4** Fish are an important food. The author supports this idea by telling us

● who eats fish.

○ where fish live.

○ how to cook fish.

**5** Why did the author *probably* write paragraph 3?

The author wanted to explain that people

have different thoughts about fish farms.

Common Core State Standards

Questions 1, 3–5: Informational Text 6. Identify the main purpose of a text, including what the author wants to answer, explain, or describe. Informational Text 8. Describe how reasons support specific points the author makes in a text. Question 2: Informational Text 1. Ask and answer such questions as *who, what, where, when, why,* and *how* to demonstrate understanding of key details in a text.

Name _____

**Read the selection. Then answer the questions that follow.**

### Earth Power

| | |
|---|---|
| Having power means being able to do something, and something that | 11 |
| has power is strong. We cannot see power, but we can see what it does. | 26 |
| A strong wind can move things as light as grass or as heavy as windmill | 41 |
| blades. A windmill is a kind of wheel that can make more power using | 55 |
| wind. A moving windmill has the power to pump water from a well. | 68 |
| Water is strong when it moves fast, and it can move things as small | 82 |
| as a leaf or as big as a boat. People also use moving water to make a | 99 |
| different kind of power, such as turning a wheel that will make power to | 113 |
| turn on lights. | 116 |
| The Earth gives us heat power, and most of it is deep inside the | 130 |
| Earth itself. We can sometimes see heat power in water that bubbles | 142 |
| up through a crack in the ground, making a hot spring. Hot water that | 156 |
| comes from the Earth gives off a gas called steam, which can also turn a | 171 |
| wheel to make more power. | 176 |
| People use a lot of power every day for such things as lights and | 190 |
| television. We should use more power from the Earth to make people's | 202 |
| lives better. | 204 |

**Turn the page.**

**Answer the questions below.**

**1** **Why did the author write the *first* paragraph?**

● to tell about wind power

○ to tell about Earth power

○ to tell about water power

**2** **Which sentence tells an opinion?**

● We should use more power from the Earth to make people's lives better.

○ A strong wind can move things as light as grass or as heavy as windmill blades.

○ The Earth gives us heat power, and most of it is deep inside the Earth itself.

**3** **The author writes paragraph 3 to tell readers about**

○ wind power.

● Earth power.

○ water power.

**4** **What is the *most likely* reason the author tells us that water power can move a boat?**

__Possible response: The author wants to__

__show how strong water power can be.__

**5** **Why does the author state that power is needed for things like lights and television?**

__The author wants us to know that people use__

__power, and we should use more Earth power.__

2 Copyright © Pearson Education, Inc., or its affiliates. All Rights Reserved.

**Common Core State Standards**

**Questions 1, 3–5: Informational Text 6.** Identify the main purpose of a text, including what the author wants to answer, explain, or describe.
**Informational Text 8.** Describe how reasons support specific points the author makes in a text. **Question 2: Informational Text 1.** Ask and answer
such questions as *who, what, where, when, why,* and *how* to demonstrate understanding of key details in a text.

Name _____

**Read the selection. Then answer the questions that follow.**

### Rainbow

| | |
|---|---:|
| There was a rainbow in the sky yesterday. Sometimes after it rains, | 12 |
| there is a rainbow. It is made of many pretty colors. They are red, | 26 |
| orange, yellow, green, blue, and purple. A rainbow is made when the sun | 39 |
| shines on small drops of water in the air. The water breaks the light into | 54 |
| the colors. For a rainbow to happen, there must be rain. There must be | 68 |
| a little sun. It is not every day that a rainbow happens. Seeing a rainbow | 83 |
| makes people happy. Rainbows are very special. Be sure to take the time | 96 |
| to see the rainbows. | 100 |

**Turn the page.**

**Answer the questions below.**

**1** **When is the best time to see a rainbow?**

○ when it is sunny

● after it rains

○ after it snows

**2** **Why does the author say that seeing a rainbow makes people happy?**

● because rainbows are beautiful

○ because rainbows mean the weather is good

○ because rainbows happen all the time

**3** **What must there be for a rainbow to happen?**

○ clouds and light

○ lightning and rain

● water and sun

**4** **Why does the author say that rainbows are special?**

The author says rainbows are special

because they do not happen every day,

and they are pretty.

2 Copyright © Pearson Education, Inc., or its affiliates. All Rights Reserved.

**Common Core State Standards**

**Questions 1, 3: Informational Text 1.** Ask and answer such questions as *who, what, where, when, why,* and *how* to demonstrate understanding of key details in a text. **Questions 2, 4: Informational Text 6.** Identify the main purpose of a text, including what the author wants to answer, explain, or describe. **Informational Text 8.** Describe how reasons support specific points the author makes in a text.

Name _____

**Read the selection. Then answer the questions that follow.**

### Tyrone's Big Meal

| | |
|---|---|
| "Those are the strangest looking pancakes I ever saw," Tyrone said | 11 |
| to his best friend. "They look like round pieces of paper." | 22 |
| "They are not pancakes," said Ingrid, "they are called crepes. We | 33 |
| made them all the time when we lived in France." | 43 |
| "It is going to take a lot of crepes to fill me up," said Tyrone as he | 60 |
| rubbed his hand in a circle on his stomach. | 69 |
| "You will be surprised. I still have to add the toppings." Ingrid | 81 |
| explained that in France crepes were served with many different | 91 |
| toppings and whipped cream. "You won't be able to eat two of them, | 104 |
| Tyrone." | 105 |
| Tyrone laughed and said, "We will see about that." Ingrid made the | 117 |
| first crepe. She loaded it with slices of apples in a sugar and cinnamon | 131 |
| sauce. Then she topped it with fresh whipped cream. Tyrone's eyes | 142 |
| opened wide when he saw it, but he ate it all. | 153 |
| Next, Ingrid made a crepe with strawberries and bananas. She topped | 163 |
| it off with powdered sugar. Tyrone did not look so happy. He took three | 176 |
| or four bites and then pushed the plate away. "You win," he said. "My | 190 |
| eyes are bigger than my stomach." | 198 |

**Turn the page.**

**Answer the questions below.**

**1** **Why did Tyrone say that the pancakes were strange?**

○ He wanted to make Ingrid laugh.

○ He wanted to eat more than one.

● He did not know what crepes were.

**2** **Why did Tyrone say it would take a lot of crepes to fill him up?**

○ Ingrid had made many crepes.

● The crepes were very thin.

○ Tyrone had not eaten breakfast.

**3** **Why did Tyrone rub his hand in a circle on his stomach?**

● to show that he could eat a lot

○ to show that he did not feel well

○ to show that he thought the crepes were round

**4** **Why did Tyrone open his eyes wide when he saw the crepe with the apples?**

○ The crepe was larger than a pancake.

● The crepe looked much bigger with the filling.

○ The crepe did not taste good with the cinnamon sauce.

**5** **What did Tyrone mean when he said, "My eyes are bigger than my stomach"?**

He thought he could eat more than he

was able to.

---

**Common Core State Standards**

**Questions 1–5: Literature 1.** Ask and answer such questions as *who, what, where, when, why,* and *how* to demonstrate understanding of key details in a text. **Literature 3.** Describe how characters in a story respond to major events and challenges.

Name _____

**Read the selection. Then answer the questions that follow.**

## It's Apple Picking Time Again

| | |
|---|---:|
| It was the first sunny day of autumn in New York. Jason and his | 14 |
| parents got into the car for the annual trip upstate. "This is my favorite | 28 |
| time of the year," said Jason. | 34 |
| "Mine too," said his mother. "It was a good season for apples. We | 47 |
| had plenty of rain and cool nights. We will be able to make delicious | 61 |
| apple pies this year." | 65 |
| They arrived at You Pick 'Em Orchard. Jason's father grabbed a long | 77 |
| pole with a small basket on the end. The basket looked a little bit like | 92 |
| a hand. "I will bring the apple picker," he said. "You know how much I | 107 |
| like the apples from the top of the tree." | 116 |
| Jason ran to the first tree he could find. He jumped up in the air and | 132 |
| grabbed as many apples as he could off of the low branches, laughing | 145 |
| the entire time. "Make sure you pick only the ripe ones," said Jason's | 158 |
| mother. "We don't want the pies to be sour." | 167 |
| Before long, they had filled two bushel baskets! "That should be | 178 |
| plenty," said Jason's father. They put the apples in the car and drove to | 192 |
| the shop to pay. Then they began the drive home. | 202 |
| Jason's parents heard a voice from the back seat. "I think I can smell | 216 |
| an apple pie baking right now." | 222 |

**Turn the page.**

**Answer the questions below.**

**1** What had made this a good year for apples?

○ the autumn

● the weather

○ the sunny day

**2** Who said, "I think I can smell an apple pie baking right now"?

○ Jason's mother

○ Jason's father

● Jason

**3** How often did Jason's family go to You Pick 'Em Orchard?

○ once

● every year

○ each spring

**4** Did Jason enjoy picking apples? Explain your answer.

Yes, because he was laughing the entire

time.

**5** What did Jason mean when he said he could almost smell the apple pie baking?

His family would soon be home baking

pies.

Common Core State Standards

Questions 1–3: Literature 1. Ask and answer such questions as *who, what, where, when, why,* and *how* to demonstrate understanding of key details in a text. Questions 4, 5: Literature 3. Describe how characters in a story respond to major events and challenges.

**Read the selection. Then answer the questions that follow.**

### Oh My!

| | |
|---|---|
| Luke and Milly went to the library. They wanted to read some books | 13 |
| about bears. Luke wanted to learn all about bears. Milly thought bears | 25 |
| were scary. | 27 |
| As Luke and Milly were looking for bear books, they heard a snuffly | 39 |
| noise. It was coming from behind the books. | 48 |
| "Do you think we hear a bear?" asked Milly. | 57 |
| "Maybe," said Luke, "if you think there are bears in the library." | 69 |
| They turned to run away and did not stop until they got home. They | 83 |
| told their father about the bear in the library. | 92 |
| Their father said, "Maybe it was Mr. Bayer, your teacher!" | 102 |

**Turn the page.**

**Answer the questions below.**

**1** **What did Luke and Milly do *first*?**

● They went to the library.

○ They talked to their father.

○ They looked at books about bears.

**2** **What is this story *mostly* about?**

○ Two children read some new books together.

○ Two children tell their dad about a bear they saw.

● Two children are scared by noises at the library.

**3** **What happened *after* Milly and Luke thought they heard a bear?**

● They ran all the way home.

○ They read the scary books.

○ They went out to the library.

**4** **What happened when Luke and Milly told their father about the bear?**

Their father told them it was probably

their teacher.

**Common Core State Standards**

**Questions 1, 3, 4: Literature 5.** Describe the overall structure of a story, including describing how the beginning introduces the story and the ending concludes the action. **Question 2: Literature 2.** Recount stories, including fables and folktales from diverse cultures, and determine their central message, lesson, or moral.

**Read the selection. Then answer the questions that follow.**

## A Winter Trip

| | |
|---|---|
| Until this year Michelle and her family had gone to Florida every | 12 |
| winter when Michelle had time off from school. Michelle thought | 22 |
| Florida was wonderful. This year, however, her father announced to the | 33 |
| family, "This year's trip will be on a ship. We are going on a ship to | 49 |
| cruise the Gulf of Mexico." | 54 |
| "I don't want to go on a ship; I want to go to Florida," Michelle said. | 70 |
| She ran into her room and cried. The more she thought about all the | 84 |
| sunny times she had had in Florida, the harder she cried. | 95 |
| Michelle's mother came into her room. "Dry your eyes," she said as | 107 |
| she smoothed Michelle's hair. "There are new and different things to do | 119 |
| on a ship." | 122 |
| The next day they boarded the ship. "It's very big," said Michelle. | 134 |
| "It is as big as three football fields," said her father and walked with | 148 |
| Michelle around the ship. | 152 |
| "Look, Dad!" exclaimed Michelle, "there's even a swimming pool!" | 161 |
| All week Michelle enjoyed the trip on the ship. | 170 |
| A week later, the ship returned. "Come on, Michelle," said her father, | 182 |
| "time to go home now." | 187 |
| "I don't want to go home," she said. "I want to stay on this ship." | 202 |

**Turn the page.**

**Answer the questions below.**

**1** What happens *before* this story begins?

- ○ Every summer Michelle's family goes camping.
- ○ Every spring Michelle's family plants new gardens.
- ● Every winter Michelle's family takes a trip to Florida.

**2** What happens *after* Michelle finds out that they are going on a ship?

- ○ She says she will be getting seasick.
- ● She says that she does not want to go.
- ○ She says she has no clothes to wear.

**3** What surprises Michelle *after* she gets on the cruise ship?

- ● She sees that the ship is a large place.
- ○ The family boards the ship with her.
- ○ Her father says the ship sails to Florida.

**4** What happens at the *end* of the story?

- ○ Michelle runs into her room and cries.
- ● Michelle does not want to leave the ship.
- ○ Michelle wants to go swimming in the pool.

**5** What is this story *mostly* about?

Michelle learns that trying something

new can be fun.

**Common Core State Standards**

**Questions 1–4: Literature 5.** Describe the overall structure of a story, including describing how the beginning introduces the story and the ending concludes the action. **Question 5: Literature 2.** Recount stories, including fables and folktales from diverse cultures, and determine their central message, lesson, or moral.

**Read the selection. Then answer the questions that follow.**

### The Turkey Bowl

| | |
|---|---|
| Thanksgiving is the day of the big town football game. For the tenth | 13 |
| year in a row, the North School and the South School football teams | 26 |
| played against each other. Since the two teams play every Thanksgiving | 37 |
| Day, the people in town smile and call it the Turkey Bowl. Everyone in | 51 |
| town goes to this important game. Even though it is not the last game of | 66 |
| the year, it is the most important game. After all, both schools are in the | 81 |
| same town, so the team that wins is the best team in town, at least for | 97 |
| a year. | 99 |
| On the opening kick-off, North School took the lead when they made | 111 |
| a touchdown. Quickly, South School tied the game with a touchdown of | 123 |
| its own. The two teams battled back and forth for the next two quarters. | 137 |
| No one scored. As the fourth quarter started, the score was still tied. | 150 |
| Finally, with one minute left to play, one of the North players ran | 163 |
| with the football into the end zone. He scored a touchdown. The crowd | 176 |
| was just so happy that either team scored; everyone jumped up and | 188 |
| down, even those who were for South School. The final seconds of the | 201 |
| game passed; North School was the winner. Its team was the best in | 214 |
| town, at least until the next Turkey Bowl. | 222 |

**Turn the page.**

**Answer the questions below.**

**1** **In this selection, what happens every year on Thanksgiving?**

○ Two football teams play their very first game of the year.

○ Two football teams play their very last game of the year.

● Two football teams play their biggest game of the year.

**2** **What happened first *after* the opening kick-off?**

○ South School dropped the football.

● North School scored a touchdown.

○ North School and South School both cheered.

**3** **How did the football game *end*?**

○ North School and South School tied.

● North School scored and won the game.

○ South School took the lead and held it.

**4** **What is this story *mostly* about?**

It tells about one of the yearly games between

two football teams in the same town.

**5** **During which quarters of the game did neither team score?**

Nobody scored during the second and third

quarters.

**Common Core State Standards**

**Questions 1, 5: Literature 1.** Ask and answer such questions as *who, what, where, when, why,* and *how* to demonstrate understanding of key details in a text. **Questions 2, 3: Literature 5.** Describe the overall structure of a story, including describing how the beginning introduces the story and the ending concludes the action. **Question 4: Literature 2.** Recount stories, including fables and folktales from diverse cultures, and determine their central message, lesson, or moral.

Name _____

**Read the selection. Then answer the questions that follow.**

### Happy Flowers

| | |
|---|---|
| Kim Anh was going to visit her grandmother. Her grandmother | 10 |
| lived in the cold mountains. Kim Anh knew that her grandmother liked | 22 |
| flowers. Before Kim Anh went into the mountains, she looked in her | 34 |
| yard for flowers to bring. | 39 |
| Kim Anh saw some grass. But grass was no good. Kim Anh wanted | 52 |
| flowers. Kim Anh saw some roses, but she did not pick those. Roses | 65 |
| could cut someone. Kim Anh saw some daisies. She thought daisies were | 77 |
| happy flowers. Kim Anh picked many daisies to take to her grandmother. | 89 |
| Happy flowers will make a happy grandmother, she thought. | 98 |

**Turn the page.**

- - - - - - - - - - - - - - - - - - - - - - - - - - - - - - - - - - - - - -

**Answer the questions below.**

**1** **How does Kim Anh think the daisies are *different* from other flowers?**

○ They are smaller, so they are easy to carry.

○ They are more colorful, yet they last longer.

● They are happy, and they cannot hurt you.

**2** **Why did Kim Anh not want to pick roses?**

○ because she thought roses were sad

● because roses might cut her finger

○ because her grandmother did not like roses

**3** **What happened at the end of the story?**

● Kim Anh picked some flowers for her grandmother.

○ Kim Anh looked for some grass for her grandmother.

○ She planted flowers in her grandmother's yard.

**4** **How do you know that Kim Anh cares for her grandmother?**

Possible response: She wants to pick flowers for grandmother to make her happy.

**Common Core State Standards**

Questions 1, 3: Literature 1. Ask and answer such questions as *who, what, where, when, why,* and *how* to demonstrate understanding of key details in a text. **Literature 5.** Describe the overall structure of a story, including describing how the beginning introduces the story and the ending concludes the action. **Questions 2, 4: Literature 3.** Describe how characters in a story respond to major events and challenges.

Name _____

**Read the selection. Then answer the questions that follow.**

### Get Well Soon

| | |
|---|---:|
| Roy looked at the seat on the bus where his best friend usually sat, | 14 |
| but it was empty. He asked everyone on the bus where Kip was, but | 28 |
| nobody knew. When Roy got to school, he learned that Kip was sick. | 41 |
| The teacher said Kip would probably be out of school for a few days. | 55 |
| Roy raised his hand. He asked the teacher if the class could make cards | 69 |
| for Kip so he would know they missed him. The teacher and the class | 83 |
| thought it was a good idea. Each child got a piece of colored paper and | 98 |
| markers. The teacher put out some fun things, such as buttons and yarn. | 111 |
| Roy cut out a face with a frown for the front of his card. He made | 127 |
| another face with a smile for the inside. He glued buttons on the faces | 141 |
| for eyes, and then he used yarn to make wild hair for both faces. They | 156 |
| looked funny, and Roy knew that Kip would laugh at the card. | 168 |
| When all the cards were finished, Roy put them together in a pile. | 181 |
| After school, he took them to Kip's house and gave them to Kip's | 194 |
| mother. Roy left hoping they would help Kip get well soon. | 205 |

**Turn the page.**

**Answer the questions below.**

**1** **When does Roy start to worry about Kip?**

● on the school bus

○ in the classroom

○ on the way home

**2** **What is Kip doing in this story?**

○ moving to a new house

● resting at home

○ visiting his grandparents

**3** **What does Roy use to make wild hair on his card?**

● yarn

○ paper

○ buttons

**4** **Roy gives all the get-well cards to**

○ Kip.

● Kip's mother.

○ Kip's teacher.

**5** **How are Roy and the other children in the class *alike*?**

They care about their friend and make

him cards.

**Common Core State Standards**

Questions 1–5: Literature 1. Ask and answer such questions as *who, what, where, when, why,* and *how* to demonstrate understanding of key details in a text.

Name _____

**Read the selection. Then answer the questions that follow.**

### Vicky's Big Day

| | |
|---|---:|
| It was an important day for Vicky. Her brother Jorge was going to | 13 |
| school with her for her last day of second grade. "I'm graduating today," | 26 |
| she told Maria Gomez, their next door neighbor. | 34 |
| "I'm extremely proud of you," said Mrs. Gomez as she waved | 45 |
| goodbye to Vicky. | 48 |
| On their way to school, Vicky and Jorge stopped at the store. Jorge | 61 |
| bought a muffin for a snack. "I'm graduating today," Vicky told the man | 74 |
| behind the counter. | 77 |
| "That's great," said the man, and he gave Vicky a cookie. | 88 |
| Vicky and her brother walked down the street. "I am graduating | 99 |
| today," Vicky informed the policeman who helped them cross the street. | 110 |
| He smiled at Vicky and said, "Good for you." | 119 |
| Finally, Vicky and Jorge arrived at school. Vicky ran into her | 130 |
| classroom to see her teacher, Mr. Peters. "Do you know what today is?" | 143 |
| he questioned Vicky. | 146 |
| "This is my big day," answered Vicky proudly. "It is my last day of | 160 |
| being in primary school. Next year I am going to be all grown up like | 175 |
| you because I will be in third grade." | 183 |
| Vicky's brother and Mr. Peters laughed. "Yes, Vicky," said Jorge, | 193 |
| "today is your big day." | 198 |

**Turn the page.**

**Answer the questions below.**

**1** **How did Vicky feel about graduating?**

● proud

○ scared

○ unhappy

**2** **Why did the man at the store give Vicky a cookie?**

○ Jorge bought the cookie.

○ The man was happy for Vicky.

● Vicky often shopped at this store.

**3** **Why did Vicky tell everyone she was graduating?**

○ She wanted to explain why Jorge was with her.

○ She thought that people did not know that she was in primary school.

● She was very happy to be going to third grade.

**4** **How are Mrs. Gomez, the man at the store, and the policeman all *alike*?**

They are all happy that Vicky is graduating.

**5** **Why did Vicky's brother and Mr. Peters laugh at the end of the story?**

She thinks she will be a grown-up next year.

2 Copyright © Pearson Education, Inc., or its affiliates. All Rights Reserved.

**Common Core State Standards**

**Questions 1–3, 5: Literature 3.** Describe how characters in a story respond to major events and challenges. **Question 4: Literature 1.** Ask and answer such questions as *who, what, where, when, why,* and *how* to demonstrate understanding of key details in a text.